EVANGELICALISM AND ANABAPTISM

EVANGELICALISM
AND
ANABAPTISM

C. Norman Kraus
Editor

HERALD PRESS
Scottdale, Pennsylvania
Kitchener, Ontario
1979

Library of Congress Cataloging in Publication Data

Main entry under title:

Evangelicalism and Anabaptism.

    "These essays were first given as addresses in
the initial Discipleship lecture forum series
(1977-78) at Goshen College."
    1. Evangelicalism—Addresses, essays, lectures.
2. Anabaptists—Addresses, essays, lectures.
I. Kraus, Clyde Norman.
BR1640.E88   270.8'2   79-12663
ISBN 0-8361-1892-8

EVANGELICALISM AND ANABAPTISM
Copyright © 1979 by Herald Press, Scottdale, Pa. 15683
Published simultaneously in Canada by Herald Press,
    Kitchener, Ont. N2G 4M5
Library of Congress Catalog Card Number: 79-12663
International Standard Book Number: 0-8361-1892-8
Printed in the United States of America
Design: Alice B. Shetler

15 14 13 12 11 10 9 8 7 6 5 4 3 2 1

Contents

Preface

Our intention in this book is to inform, clarify, and evaluate. None of the writers attempts to make the case for or against either Evangelicalism or Anabaptism, although personal viewpoints do, and should, come through in a series of this kind. Some of the writers, in fact, would identify themselves as being both evangelical and Anabaptist. We are trying to place the two movements side by side for comparative analysis and critical evaluation in an attempt to understand our present perspectives on scriptural interpretation and application today.

Perhaps a word should be said about the use of the term "Anabaptist." In its historical use it describes a sixteenth-century radical reform movement which called for fundamental changes in the church and society based on a fresh understanding of the New Testament. It offered a more radical biblical critique than either Luther or any other Reformer. On particular issues, there was great variation among Anabaptists. It was a dynamic, often uncoordinated movement and not a carefully reasoned theological-ethical position. Thus we use the term generically today to describe a position that appeals to the New Testament as the final authority for Christians, that calls for radical discipleship under the lordship of Jesus Christ, that offers a radical critique of the social order, and calls the world to repentence and new life in the kingdom of God. All the authors have attempted to bring this perspective to bear on their examination of Evangelicalism.

These essays were first given as addresses in the initial Discipleship Lecture Forum Series (1977-78) at Goshen College. The series, sponsored by the Center for Discipleship, was planned for a general audience. The lectures were substantive but popular in form, and each one was followed by extensive discussion.

It is my hope that the original hearers and now the readers of this book will be stimulated to a fresh examination of the contemporary issues facing the church and the teachings of Holy Scripture.

C. Norman Kraus
Center for Discipleship
1978

CHAPTER 1

Introduction:
What Is Evangelicalism?

C. Norman Kraus

American Evangelicalism is a post-fundamentalist movement. The Evangelicals are not reconstructed liberals. These are called neoorthodox or neoliberal. Neither do they represent a resurgence of middle-of-the-road Protestant denominationalism. The denominational tide is ebbing. They are the descendants and heirs of Fundamentalism, and that fact definitely shapes the nature of the issues that are central to the movement as well as the piety and lifestyle that characterize it.

To be precise one must speak of "American Evangelicalism" to designate the contemporary movement because the word evangelical has a much broader historical usage. In the first place it comes from the New Testament word which is translated "gospel." The evangel is the good news. In the Reformation era the Protestants and Anabaptists thought of themselves as evangelicals because they taught salvation by grace—the evangel—in

---

C. Norman Kraus is professor of religion and director of the Center for Discipleship at Goshen College. His most recent book is *The Authentic Witness* (Eerdmans, 1979).

contrast to a salvation by works which they associated
with Roman Catholicism. So the Lutheran Church in
Germany was called the Evangelical Church.

In the eighteenth and nineteenth centuries when Rationalism, Liberalism, and Modernism emerged in
Protestant churches, the orthodox party, which came to
be called Fundamentalism in America, claimed that
liberals were no longer evangelical because they had
diluted the doctrines of sin and grace. Liberals rejected
doctrines like the penal atonement and a supernatural
conversion; they believed in the essential goodness of
human nature, and in the possibility of progress toward
the kingdom of God through dedicated, rational human
effort. In this way the term evangelical came to be more
closely associated with the fundamentalists. It should be
pointed out, however, that there were a great many
people who did not identify with Fundamentalism, but
who were and considered themselves to be evangelical.
One can even speak of the evangelical liberals—those
who remained Christ-centered and held firmly to salvation by grace through faith, but who were also willing to
adapt their theology to the new findings of science.

Fundamentalism developed as a defensive reaction to
Liberalism. (See chapter 3.) It insisted upon the
Protestant scholastic theory of biblical authority based on
verbal inspiration and the absolute inerrancy of Scripture. Further, it stressed the supernatural character of
the spiritual new birth in contrast to what it considered a
doctrine of salvation by religious conditioning. The so-
called "fundamentals" were all beliefs that emphasized
the *supernatural* essence of Christianity, and they were
based upon a literalistic, rational interpretation of the
"inerrant Scripture."

Beside these things, which would also characterize Protestant Orthodoxy, Fundamentalism accepted the Plymouth Brethren concept of a dispensational interpretation of Scripture which was expounded in the notes of the *Scofield Reference Bible* (1909). This system of interpretation took a very pessimistic view of the church. It held that the vast majority of the churches—"Christendom"—was apostate. It called for individual Christians to separate themselves from the churches into fellowships of true believers awaiting the imminent return of Christ. It despaired of any social improvement through the work of the Holy Spirit in the world. It identified the kingdom of God with a totally future Jewish millennium. All its emphasis was placed upon snatching individual souls from hell fire. Thus its focal concern was on "personal evangelism" that called for men and women to be "born again," and get ready for a future millennial kingdom which Christ would establish instead of living a kingdom style life here and now.

Under the impact of such defensive and negative influences Fundamentalism tended toward a separatist or sectarian stance, an oversimplified view of the issues involved, and an exaggerated sense of its own critical importance to the preservation of true doctrine. Fundamentalists tended to be highly suspicious of anyone who did not accept their doctrinal defintions.

During the period immediately following World War II a number of significant developments took place that pointed toward a resurgence of conservative Protestantism. The formation of the National Association of Evangelicals in 1942-43 laid the groundwork for what was to follow. This organization was formed to provide a basis of cooperation for those conservative Protestants who could not in good faith work with the more liberal Federal Council of Churches.[1] On the other side, however, it explicitly rejected the possibility of joining the newly formed American Council of Christian Churches (1941) which was loudly calling for an aggressive, separatist fundamentalist organization. It called for unified, dynamic, cooperative programs—such as evangelism, Christian education, relations with government, and foreign missions—based on traditional evangelical beliefs. Its statement of faith obviously side-stepped the more technical aspects of the biblical inerrancy debate by leaving out the word inerrancy and the phrase "verbal and plenary" inspiration. It also omitted reference to the premillennial second coming of Christ; and it included a positive statement on the "spiritual unity of believers."

Many related activities and organizations sprang up thereafter. *Youth for Christ* was organized in 1944, the *Evangelical Foreign Missions Association* formed in 1945, and the year following the *World Relief Commission* of the NAE was organized. In 1947 *Fuller Theological Seminary* was founded. The younger scholars who joined the Fuller faculty were to become the leaders of the new Evangelical theological revival. In 1949 the *Evangelical Theological Society* was formed. The single theological requirement for joining this society was a belief in the inerrancy of Scripture. That same year a young evangelist named Billy Graham first came into national prominence. On every front the Evangelicals were beginning to take a newly aggressive and organized stance.

This new post-Fundamentalist movement clearly sought both continuity and discontinuity with its predecessor. It forthrightly claimed to stand for all the fundamental doctrines, but it wished to demonstrate a new spirit of tolerance within "evangelical" limits, and a broadened concern for the life and mission of the churches. It clearly represented a more ambitious theological and ecclesiastical coalition than Fundamentalism had been able to effectively organize, but it built on that movement's precedents. Because of its broader sympathies the more strict Fundamentalists became suspicious of it.

While Evangelicalism stands in continuity with Fundamentalism, many of its spokesmen have been critical of Fundamentalism's narrowness of vision and its defensive, suspicious stance. They have criticized it as too separatist (sectarian) in its ecclesiology, too individualistic in its ethics, too futuristic in its eschatology, too simplistic in its theology, and too combative in its spirit. Not until very recently, however, have Fundamentalism's basic doctrinal positions begun to be questioned. Most Evangelicals have loudly proclaimed their full allegiance to the "fundamentals of the faith."

In 1947 Carl F. H. Henry, one of the new evangelical breed, published *The Uneasy Conscience of Fundamentalism* criticizing fundamentalists for their lack of social consciousness. If we may skip ahead some two decades, we see the outcome of this initial revisionism in the formation of the "Evangelicals for Social Action."

In 1952 another young Fuller professor, George E. Ladd, published *Crucial Questions about the Kingdom of God* challenging the dispensationalist doctrines of C. I. Scofield. Ladd still held himself to be a premillennialist, but he repudiated Darbyite additions like the secret rapture. Wilbur Smith, one of the old guard who was also on the Fuller faculty at the time, asked his brothers and sisters to give the young biblical scholar a hearing although he himself did not go along with the revisionism. Again skipping ahead, the rejection of the dispensational scheme of Bible interpretation has become a characteristic of the new Evangelical theological stance.

In his small book *Evangelical Responsibility in Contemporary Theology* (1957) Carl Henry spoke of the "Fundamentalist reduction" of theology and called it a "distinctly twentieth-century expression of Christianity. . . ." That same year a symposium of evangelical scholars was published entitled *Contemporary Evangelical Theology*. Both of these volumes clearly indicate that these new Evangelicals had rediscovered with great appreciation the earlier conservative tradition represented in men like A. H. Strong (Baptist), Charles Hodge and B. B. Warfield (Presbyterian), and James Orr (Presbyterian from Scotland). One might speak of this as the rediscovery of the great tradition of Conservative Protestant systematic theology. Carnell's *The Case for Orthodox Theology* (1959) and some of Bernard Ramm's books clearly identify Evangelical theology with this broader, more profound tradition of orthodox theology.

This new theological interest led to a conscious attempt to expand the discussions still farther. *Christianity Today* was begun in 1956 as a vehicle for Evangelical dialogue. Also in the mid-fifties younger Evangelical scholars began to study the works of neoorthodox theologians like Karl Barth and Emil Brunner and to analyze them with critical appreciation. (Indeed, Carl Henry admitted privately that the writings of Barth and Brunner furnished the real stimulation for him—not, of course, that he agreed with them!) Up to that time, these men had simply been ignored as "new modernists." At about the same time the *American Scientific Affiliation,* a society for evangelical scientists which had been founded in 1941, took a new look at old scientific questions and came up with new conclusions about the age of the earth and the process called evolution. They argued that their new findings could be harmonized with a proper understanding of the biblical accounts. After all, a generation earlier the great defender of orthodox doctrine, B. B. Warfield, had pointed out that the new evidence for the antiquity of the human species in no way contradicted Scripture.

All this time Billy Graham's influence was burgeoning as he was developing a multimillion dollar radio and television empire. New evangelical seminaries and colleges were being started. On the foreign mission front new aggressive interdenominational organizations were being formed. *World Vision* was begun by the evangelist Bob Pierce in 1950 as an evangelical child care agency. It has since become a major evangelical agency dispensing emergency aid, promoting community development and evangelism as well as supplying money to take care of needy children. (Over one half of its budget is still given to child care.) *MAP International* was organized to dispense medical supplies and relief (1954). In 1951 a new flashy evangelistic venture called *Campus Crusade* was organized under the leadership of former businessman and marketing executive, Bill Bright, and soon it was competing with the older *Inter-Varsity Christian Fellowship* on college campuses. IVCF itself began an expanded publication program and sponsored the huge mission rallies for young people at Urbana, Illinois.

The most recent major developments are the international conferences on evangelism and world mission held in Berlin (1966) and Lausanne (1974). These conferences attracted a wide spectrum of "evangelicals" indeed, and now a continuation committee growing out of the Lausanne conference is at work to further guide and coordinate the world mission of Evangelicalism.[2] One cannot help but note how similar are these developments to those a half century or so earlier that finally gave birth to the World Council of Churches.

Along with this burgeoning growth of organization and activity we should note also the change in the public climate and attitude toward religion and its public expression. The new interest and acceptance extends to all religious groups, but the evangelicals have obviously made the most of it. Evangelical religious experience and convictions are freely talked about on the public talk shows and in major secular publications. Evangelical religious books have become best sellers, and in some cases have made their authors millionaires. "Christian Yellow Pages" featuring "born again" merchants became a commercial venture. Twenty-four hour religious radio stations, and more recently religious television stations, have become money-makers. Pat Boone, Anita Bryant, Chuck Colson, and Eldridge Cleaver are a mere sample of famous personalities who have lent their names and prestige to further the movement. Undoubtedly they have a genuine religious experience, but the point here is their forthright and aggressive public identification with the movement.

This shift in public opinion had begun already in the early 1970s. It was heralded by the "Honor America" celebration on July Fourth, 1970, when Billy Graham was featured as the star speaker along with Bob Hope and John Wayne in a mass gathering on the Washington, D.C., mall. It came to a political climax in the 1976 elections when even the candidates' "born again" status became a political issue. The candidates went out of their way to affirm their evangelical religious stance. But by 1978 it does not seem to have much abated, for a national poll taken that spring indicated that 34 percent of adult Americans claim to be "born again" Christians![3]

So at the moment, 1978, Evangelicalism is in the ascendency in America, but has it already peaked or are the tensions obvious in the movement merely the growing pains of youth? Serious theological tensions and conflicts have indeed developed, but as J. Lawrence Burkholder points out Evangelicalism is still a power to be reckoned with.

Central to much of the controversy in Evangelicalism is the question of inerrancy. An old guard led by men who were at the center of the movement a decade ago have mounted a campaign to hold the line on strict inerrancy. This renewal of the inerrancy debate, which had been going on below the surface for a number of years, erupted when Harold Lindsell published his *The Battle for The Bible* in 1976. The debate is over how precisely the term inerrant is to be applied to Scripture. Does it necessitate a scientific accuracy in all data reported? Or should it be interpreted as giving infallible authority to the central message of Scripture—in the words of the time-honored phrase "the infallible rule *for faith and practice*"? This debate has given rise to a new term, "non-inerrancy," a term to distinguish evangelicals who do not hold to strict inerrancy from the liberals who accept the idea that there is error in the scriptural records.

The issue came to a head in the Evangelical Theolog-

ical Society in 1977-78 when action was brought to expel
a member who held to the "non-inerrancy" theory on
the grounds that it did not meet the society's requirement of belief in the inerrant Scripture. Then in the fall
of 1977 the International Council of Biblical Inerrancy
was formed by thirty prominent evangelical leaders. Its
stated purpose is to "educate the evangelical community
about the doctrine's [inerrancy] importance, to show that
those who deny inerrancy are 'out of step' with the Bible
and the historic evangelical mainstream," and to effect
"institutional changes within seminaries, denominations,
mission agencies, and other Christian organizations."[4]

J. C. Wenger discusses the issue giving historical background and evaluation (Chapter 6). He concludes that
the strict inerrantists are in danger of a docetic view of
Scripture, that is, not properly recognizing the human as
well as the divine element in Scripture, but he strongly
affirms the infallible authority of the Bible for faith and
life. In this he has clearly taken his stand with the
classical Reformers including Menno Simons.

As we noted, the eschatology question has also become
a tension point within the movement. In the mid-fifties a
blue-ribbon group of dispensationalist scholars—Allan
MacRae, Wilbur M. Smith, and John F. Walvoord,
among others—began the revision of the *Scofield
Reference Bible*. The revision was finally published in
1967 after ten years of work. One might have expected
this first revision of Scofield in fifty years to have been
hailed as a major scholarly event, but it was received with
very mixed feelings. On the one hand, in spite of the fact
that no issues of substance were changed, the very idea of
a revision disturbed many. Even this updating to clear up
misunderstandings that had been fostered by some of

Scofield's vocabulary seemed sacrilege. On the other hand, a significant number of evangelical scholars showed little interest because they had already rejected the older Dispensationalism altogether.

While this debate goes on at the scholarly level men like Hal Lindsey and David Wilkerson have captured the popular imagination with books and films that predict cataclysmic catastrophe in the near future and the "secret rapture" of the faithful in an unobserved coming of Jesus for His saints. Lindsey's *The Late Great Planet Earth*, first published in 1970, has sold millions; and Wilkerson's "vision" in print and on film has held these same millions spellbound with expectancy and dread. It matters little that evangelical biblical scholars repudiate their books as shallow at best and heretical at worst.

In chapter 7 Marlin Jeschke explores this element of the evangelical mix. He points out that dispensational theology is a relatively new arrival on the evangelical scene, although in mood and apocalyptic content it has its earlier counterparts. While it is popular at the moment, he feels that Hal Lindsey's interpretation has a fadist quality which makes it suspect even on its face.

Just as the theological scope of Evangelicalism has been broadened so also have its political and social views. Fundamentalists were, by and large, also politically "right wing," in fact, often even "far right." They strictly separated religion and politics in theory, but in the name of God-given moral laws they usually defended the status quo in the societal order, and they interpreted laissez faire capitalism and the sacred right of private property as the direct implication of the eighth commandment. Now wide cracks have begun to appear in Evangelicalism's political and social front.

In fact, within the Evangelical movement a wide variety of opinion on social and political issues exists. Evangelical periodicals are publishing articles by Evangelicals
calling for open-minded examination of the issues involved in homosexuality and the application of biblical
teaching to them as well as articles flatly denouncing homosexuality as sin and perversion in the name of the Bible. Evangelicals are on both sides of the women's rights
issue. Although most evangelicals are still sympathetic
with militarism, there are loud persistent voices among
them calling for a consistent biblical pacifism. Political
differences showed plainly when in the 1976 presidential
campaign many Evangelicals with right-wing political
convictions found themselves quite unhappy with some
of the "born-again" candidates.[5] The tension arises when
both sides identify their positions with biblical and
theological orthodoxy.

John Lapp analyzes this variety of opinion in chapter
5. Lapp points out that the political right has three major
characteristics: anticommunism, a conspiracy view of
history, and extreme pessimism about the future. These
views are very compatible with the older fundamentalist
theology represented by men like Billy James Hargis and
Carl McIntire. While many neo-Evangelicals would
understand and sympathize with these views, few take
the "doomsday" route of the John Birch Society or
McIntire's "Twentieth-Century Reformation."

The broad political middle of Evangelicalism can still
be described as committed to individualism, private
property, free enterprise capitalism, and political democracy. They want a legal separation of church and
state, but at the same time see no problem in a religious
majority legislating a religiously based morality for the

good of the nation. Surveys indicate that Billy Graham functions as something of a political bellwether for this centrist majority.

But the younger radical Evangelicals who have been profoundly influenced by the concepts of Anabaptism are raising a spirited challenge to this middle-of-the-road identification of Christian discipleship and "the American way of life." These radical voices are represented in the essays of West Michaelson and Ron Sider. Michaelson, managing editor of *Sojourners*, calls Evangelicals to a costly discipleship which identifies with and seeks justice for the exploited (chapter 4). Sider, president of the Evangelicals for Social Action, echoes this call. He insists that *orthopraxy* and *orthodoxy* must be kept together, and he challenges Mennonites, who are the descendants of the Anabaptists, to join the Evangelical movement both in order to challenge and be challenged by it (chapter 8).

Evangelicalism, then, is a highly varigated coalition of Christians who stand in the tradition of seventeenth- and eighteenth-century Protestant Orthodoxy. That movement was divided into its pietistic and scholastic factions, but both groups held fast to biblical authority whether they defined it in rational theological terms or as a spiritual and moral guide which provided a discipline for Christian experience and life. Both groups identified with the national churches and felt secure in the context of a christianized social order. Even the "free churches" did not seriously challenge the concept of a Christian base for social and political order.

Today these same elements seem to give the movement its cohesion. Insistence on biblical authority however it may be interpreted, evangelism as the central purpose of the church, the experience of "born-again" religion, and a large dose of good old-fashioned Americanism hold it together despite its stresses and strains.

CHAPTER 2

Popular Evangelicalism:
An Appraisal

J. Lawrence Burkholder

This essay attempts to make a descriptive analysis of popular Evangelicalism as a socio-religious phenomenon. Evangelicalism is viewed here as a historical movement subject to the contingencies of all historical developments. Although we cannot fully "explain" the evangelical phenomenon within the mysteries of the providential order, nevertheless it may be helpful to make a modest historical examination and critique of the movement. There are, after all, also many human factors at work in this complex social development.

The word "evangelical" is ambiguous. It comes from the New Testament word which means "the good news," and it is in the first instance an adjective to describe that which pertains to or is characterized by the gospel. Thus by definition in the generic sense, all Christians are evangelical.

But there are more specific uses. In Europe, the word

J. Lawrence Burkholder is professor of Bible and philosophy and president of Goshen College. Formerly a professor at Harvard University, he is a popular teacher at church conferences.

evangelical has been synonymous with Protestant. However, in America "evangelical" points to a complex, highly differentiated, religio-sociological development, largely within but not limited to Protestantism, with its own language, mannerism, political bias, piety, theological interpretation, self-consciousness and institutional bases. Some denominations are evangelical; others contain an evangelical wing.

It should be made clear at the outset that the Evangelical movement is complex and for that reason one is hard pressed to characterize the movement as a whole. Certainly one must distinguish between popular Evangelicals and evangelical denominations that are deeply rooted in historic Protestantism and in Reformation theologies. If, for example, one refers to our Christian Reformed brothers and sisters as "evangelicals," one must distinguish them from the devotees of popular Evangelicalism. The Reformed Church is committed to a learned ministry, a carefully considered theology, a great history, a high view of the church, and a thoughtful approach to culture. The Christian Reformed Church may be said to be evangelical in a classic Protestant sense by reason of its conservative theology, traditional worship, and serious attitude toward life.

Popular Evangelicalism by contrast is a religious phenomenon with few historic roots, relatively few traditional denominational ties and for the most part with unsophisticated theologies. Although popular Evangelicals speak about the "old-time religion" and make almost continuous references to the past, popular Evangelicalism is heavily impacted by contemporary values, manners, and prejudices.

Popular Evangelicalism is evangelical in the sense that

its theology is fundamental, or orthodox, and its practice is evangelistic. It is popular in the sense that it appeals to a major segment of the population and it identifies with prevailing values.

One thing sure, Evangelicalism is a power to be reckoned with. It can no longer be consigned to the backwaters of American religion. When 34 percent of adult Americans claim to be "born again" and 46 percent of the Protestants believe that the Bible should be taken literally, you can be certain that Evangelicalism is today more representative of American Protestantism than has generally been assumed.

Evangelicals have captured the word "Christian" while the major denominations have preferred to use less explicit and more ambiguous language. Indeed, in many circles, the adjective Christian has become synonymous with Evangelical. When Christian is used to describe colleges, business associations, basketball teams, broadcasting stations, publishing houses, and camps, you may be sure that it is being used as an Evangelical shibboleth.

For Evangelicals making Christianity overt is an implication of the missionary mandate. To be reserved in matters pertaining to Christianity is to be less than true to Christ and the gospel. When speaking of the faith, Evangelicals tend to speak directly and unambiguously even if the language is repetitive. They are not likely to talk about their religious background but rather about their present commitment to Christ. They downgrade denominational preferences as misplaced loyalties. They are "born again" and not simply "brought up." Frequently they avoid the term "religion" as too nebulous, and the demand for specificity reinforces Jesus-Christ-talk even in preference to God-talk. To speak about Christ freely and openly, especially within secular contexts generally reserved for other matters, is to be Evangelical.

Furthermore, Evangelicals have captured the word "world." Whether in the form of *world* vision, *world* evangelism, or *world* missionary press, the world is the frame of reference for even the smallest of missionary enterprises. This is symptomatic of more than a romantic ideal or an exaggerated sense of importance. It reflects a stage in missionary consciousness once characteristic of main-line Protestantism but subsequently abandoned in the face of modern historical developments.

Evangelicalism has retained one of the basic elements of the vision of John R. Mott, namely, hope for the redemption of the world—if not in "this generation." Whereas main-line churches have abandoned, for all practical purposes, expectations of global effectiveness, Evangelical Christians cling to the hope that converts will be sufficient in number and influence to justify their evangelistic efforts premised upon the second coming of Christ. Hence, mass evangelism, "crusade" after "crusade," Bible smuggling, ever more translations of Scripture, high-powered radio and television stations, projected multimillion dollar world evangelism centers! Evangelicals may be said to have retained, however altered, the vision, the hope, and the commitment of the modern missionary movement. Whereas main-line churches have retreated in the face of resurgent nationalism, secularism, and regional cultural consciousness, Evangelicals press the claims of Christ relatively unimpeded by modernity.

Complex organization and programming are a third characteristic of Evangelicalism. It is highly institutionalized. No longer is the movement carried by the faith and life of unselfconscious, lower class, working, and hill people whose identity is supplied by folk traditions, revivalism and family ties. In recent years, it has adapted to the ways of the world and has exploited the power of institutionalized religion. It is the only segment of the American religion that makes significant use of the electronic media. It has organized, however tenuously, an "electronic church" consisting of millions of people whose affiliation is achieved by contributions to powerful radio preachers and personalities. Evangelical broadcasting has replaced a great tradition of radio preaching by such liberals of the thirties as Harry Emerson Fosdick and Ralph Sockman. One may not be impressed by the quality of radio preaching today, but a sweep of the dial indicates that Evangelicals dominate the airwaves.

The tendency of Evangelicals to create Christian institutional alternatives to the dominant institutions of America is referred to technically as "institutional parallelism." This takes the form of Christian elementary schools, Christian college consortia, Christian publishing companies, Christian basketball leagues, Christian travel bureaus, and even Christian "yellow pages." The institutionalization of Evangelicalism is a concomitant of the movement of farm and working people into the middle class. As they moved up the ladder, they took their religion along with them. By combining numbers, zeal, and money, Evangelicals have established an amazing power base.

In recent years, they have devoloped a consciousness of political power. For the first time in many decades the United States has a self-acknowledged "born-again" president whose policies may not accord in all respects with evangelical predilections, but whose position symbolizes a growing political consciousness of a traditionally nonpolitical, if not anti-political segment of the religious spectrum.

One also notes that the Evangelicals take the religious and theological insights of main-line churches and give them popular expressions. For example, such concepts as "dialogue," "the small group," and "lay ministry" which first found their post-World War II religious expressions among the "Evangelical Academies" of Europe, the World Council of Churches, and the National Council of Churches, have now found their concrete applications in highly organized interdenominational neighborhood prayer groups, "Full Gospel" businessmen's groups, TV talk shows, and prayer breakfasts. One may rue the popularization and sometimes the trivialization of theological insights of the post-World War II crisis theology, but one cannot understand the Evangelical movement without recognizing, on the one hand, the dependence of Evangelicals upon the theological creativity of the liberals and, on the other hand, their access to the people.

Evangelical power is expressed in numbers. Evangelicals measure their effectiveness by the numbers of people who attend church, the size of the "listening audience," the number of converts, the number and size of church buses, the size of the Sunday school offering, the number of missionaries on the field. The criteria for success are similar to the criteria used by business.

Even though the tendency among Evangelicals to measure success by numbers may appear somewhat crass, it is hard to distinguish it from the dominant motif of Liberalism of an earlier period. At the beginning of the twentieth century it was success-oriented liberals who optimistically called it *The Christian Century*. Who can deny that the motif of cathedral-like downtown churches of the earlier part of this century spoke of a tie between the growth of capitalism and main-line churches. If the Evangelicals overdo the numbers game, it is a game learned from older liberal pros whose arthritic joints bespeak of the same spirit of success.

Historical Factors in Evangelical Success

How shall we explain the success of Evangelicalism at this stage in history? We need not be so presumptuous as to interpret Evangelicalism in relation to the purposes of God. There are less obscure reasons on the historical plane, inadequate as they may be.

First of all, popular evangelical religion legitimizes and indeed expresses the values of American culture. Evangelicalism is the religious counterpart to a conservative cultural mood. It upholds the preservation of the American dream and opposition to external and internal enemies. Evangelicalism represents today a curious blend of conformity and nonconformity. Historically Evangelicals have been nonconformists. Their roots are sectarian and their social position has until recent times reinforced nonconformist attitudes. But with post-World War II upward mobility, their social position has made them participants in the American dream. This has meant that their relationship to the culture has changed fundamentally, and the content of their social criticism has changed accordingly. Whereas their earlier attitudes emanated from the consciousness of the dispossessed and were directed against the powerful (city people, Wall Street, the Eastern establishment, political leaders,

Hollywood, and foreigners) now they are directed against those who would threaten the establishment (communists, radicals, liberals, and homosexuals).

Evangelicals are, therefore, in the enviable position of aligning themselves with the deepest desires of this generation for freedom, prosperity, enterprise, individualism, private ownership, family, and good clean living. These are seen to be grounded unambiguously in the law of God and the providential ordering of history. No one should underestimate the power which emanates from the coincidence of human aspirations and religious sanctions. It is difficult to resist those who are for what people want and who are against "sin" at the same time.

The identification of Providence with American history is, of course, not new. The American dream has always had a religious component. It is religious in the sense that it has been seen as an extension of the history of Israel and the theology of the people of God. To be sure the roots of the American dream go back to ideas of the Enlightenment and democracy but they are entwined with the idea of a holy nation. In Evangelicalism these are fused to the degree that the founders of the nation have been confused with the fathers of the faith. Current failures of the nation are interpreted as a falling away from the faith. The role of evangelical preachers is to call the nation back to its primal holiness and providential meaning.

If popular Evangelicalism appears dangerously simplistic, it may be recalled that the evangelical interpretation of American history is not without its parallels among the main-line churches of a previous generation. Liberalism as expressed in the Social Gospel also operated upon the premise of the unity of religion and society. In the pre-World War II period, the fusion of the industrial growth, evolution, scientific progress, education, the growth of cities and institutional development not only supplied the conceptual framework for American Christianity but was also offered as a model for China and other nations to which thousands of missionaries preached the Social Gospel.

The American dream as set forth by Liberalism, however, died following World War I. It was crushed by the impact of a series of catastrophies and unexpected developments such as the depression, World War II, the Nazi death camps, resurgent nationalism and complexity. It declined also because its own prophetic impulses turned upon itself and accused it of pride, presumption, and premature thoughts about the location and meaning of divine judgment.

The real difference between the liberal and evangelical participation in the American dream is the role of prophecy. Liberalism was grounded in Hebrew prophecy and its dream was the dream of Amos for a just society. It interpreted Jesus primarily as a Prophet whose teaching lay within the possibilities of individuals and institutions. Its rendition of the American dream was a variation upon the theme of the kingdom of God. By contrast, popular Evangelicalism contains virtually no prophetic elements. It is essentially priestly insofar as it is oriented toward the maintenance of the social order, the forgiveness of individual sins, and individual personal ministries. Evangelicalism would call our attention to sin, but sin is understood largely as personal transgressions and the structures of society as such are seldom criticized. Evangelicalism is a static interpretation of Christianity within which Jesus is presented as an eternal Mediator and Savior. Its scriptural appeal is to those passages which speak of individual rational or intellectual response (knowledge) to a verbal message. And among its historical precedents is Gnosticism of which Evangelicalism is a somewhat crude and popular rendition.

As carriers of the American dream Evangelicals have accepted and have indeed exploited current cultural idiom and the popular demeanor. They have learned from show business and the advertizing media. Their demeanor, dress, ubiquitous smiles, extroversion, and southern accents seem to reflect an inordinate desire to get with it. Evangelical churches do not require ordinary people to change in order to be accepted. They are warned against drinking and swearing but the cross is seldom referred to as a component of the Christian life. To accept Christ is to repent of one's sins but the expectations that follow are seldom of a nature that places one at odds with the society at large. In fact, for many people being "born again" is to move from the fringes toward the center of the community life. The new birth is a rite of passage into American society. It is to move from marginal existence into the cultural stream with the approval of the community. It is to discover the terms within which the benefits of the American dream may be realized. It is to be introduced to the possibility of success.

Another reason for success of the evangelicals is the simplicity of its message. Popular evangelical preaching is seldom analytical. Its appeal is due to its ability to present the "truth" without qualification, hesitation, elaboration, nuance, or subtlety. It is direct, simple, dogmatic, and safely within the bounds of popular prejudices. As far as the message goes, it can be understood.

Remarkably little Bible content is to be found in evangelical preaching. There are numerous references to the Bible as the Word of God, but seldom is the Bible exposited thoroughly and thoughtfully. But this generation prefers not to be reminded of unsolvable problems, painful dilemmas, inscrutable mysteries, and depressing prospects. People want certainty and someone who speaks with authority.

Another reason for the success of the Evangelicals is their evangelistic zeal. They are the people who get out Sunday morning to bus them in. They are the people who broadcast their Sunday morning services. Sometimes they tithe. They hold Wednesday evening prayer meetings. They are open to everyone. The legacy of traditional denominational designations is avoided by such unimposing names for churches as "Free Gospel," "Calvary Temple," "Bible Church," and "Grace Tabernacle." And everyone is designated a soul winner—not just the minister who, curiously enough, is frequently an authoritarian figure.

Finally, the Evangelicals are benefiting from a conservative backlash resulting from the revolutionary activities of the 1960s. It is well known that the main-line churches became deeply involved in the social upheavals occasioned by civil rights and opposition to the Vietnam War. Major denominations were divided, resulting not only in crises within local congregations but divisions between denominational headquarters and the grass roots. Contributions dropped off as members struggled over the role of prophetic witness, social action, civil disobedience, and patriotism.

The Evangelicals were largely spared such internal conflicts up to the present. They were conservative in their identifications with the *status quo*. Therefore, they were ready to move intact when the mood of the nation moved in a more conservative direction. To be sure most evangelicals have in recent years internalized many of the revolutionary changes of the 1960s. But they were spared the price of prophetic witness.

One may say that as a general rule evangelicals have incorporated change after the initial shock has been absorbed by the major denominations. This pattern is true not only with respect to social change but with theological development. When one recalls the resistance of conservatives to the Revised Standard Version of the Bible in the 1950s, it is curious that the Evangelicals would at a later date identify so totally and uncritically with a paraphrase such as *The Living Bible*. And when it comes to major theological movements it is remarkable how Evangelicals have latched on to the ideas of Brunner and Barth after some 40 years. This suggests that the strength of Evangelicals is the strength of social and intellectual lag. Those who win the masses are not always the avant-garde. There are times when populations that have been thrust from one historical situation into another look to religion not for new ideas but for security. This is what the Evangelicals offer by their simple, authoritative, reassuring identification with the people.

Evangelicalism's Spiritual Integrity

But as we have indicated earlier, the success of the Evangelicals is not simply due to a coincidence of religious and national moods. To be fair, one must acknowledge that Evangelical theology and piety must be taken seriously as an interpretation of the gospel with integrity and historical precedent. When radio preachers and club personalities offer salvation in a moment and at a distance by simply "surrendering your life to Jesus," one may be offended by its crass superficiality. However, at its best, Evangelical preaching must be interpreted as a simple and popular rendition of a classical interpretation of Christianity.

It is an interpretation that appeared in early Christianity when in response to the failure of an immediate parousia (the second coming of Christ) the Christian community became increasingly concerned about how to come to terms with universal experience. As the hope of a "new heaven and a new earth" receded or was projected into an unknown future, the gospel was interpreted increasingly in non-historical terms. This tendency appears in the *Gospel of John* where the figure of Jesus is clothed in mystery, and the kingdom is not "of this world." Salvation as "a new creation," to use a Pauline phrase, was reinterpreted to mean a new being in relation to the permanent structure of existence and not a radically new social situation. Hence, salvation was redefined as the answer to personal guilt, suffering, death, and deliverance from the consequences of living as a creature in a threatening world. Evangelical theology is rooted in an interpretation of the gospel that concentrates more upon the need for personal salvation than social change.

Thus when the popular evangelists give the invitation to accept Christ, however stereotyped and professional, they are bringing to ordinary people, young and old, a solution to their deepest problems. They need to be rescued from guilt, loneliness, broken relationship, insecurity, doubt, and rejection. When "Jesus saves," He saves one not from minor embarrassment but from total failure and a feeling of damnation.

Therefore, if one can look beneath the surface of popular Evangelical preaching, one finds a theological framework with historical precedent and integrity. This would account in considerable measure for its success. People are saved from the problems of humanity that transcend historical accident.

One should also acknowledge the fact that Evangelical churches represent one of the most significant components in the moral education of the common people and especially children. Church buses, of which there are thousands, bring children from broken homes, rough neighborhoods, alcoholism, and violence to a school of elementary morality. Here a vision of harmony, stability, and goodness is presented. Here children receive their earliest moral training. For many young people this is the only opportunity that they have to transcend their environment. In this respect the Evangelical churches make a major contribution to society—a contribution for which they are given inadequate recognition.

When it comes to the future prospects of the Evangelical movement, it is easy to predict that there will be continued differentiation on the basis of historical precedent. The word "evangelical" is already so ambiguous as to call into question its utility. Many individuals and some denominations that once preferred to be called evangelical rather than fundamentalist now question their identification with the word. Certainly it is necessary to distinguish between various groups of Evangelicals with reference to theological emphasis, piety, social consciousness, historical identity, and cultural accommodation. Be that as it may, the impact of Evangelicalism is significant and the main-line churches need to ponder whether the vitality of the Evangelical movement is to be interpreted as providential or simply as a continuation of a trend toward individualism and the dissolution of traditional historic Christianity into spiritual flotsam on the tides of cultural change.

CHAPTER 3

Evangelicalism: The Great Coalition

C. Norman Kraus

Contemporary American Evangelicalism is a diverse and conglomerate coalition of conservative Protestants, and, some might even add Roman Catholic, charismatics. I think we might better comprehend the situation if we picture the two overlapping groups within the broad movement under two umbrellas which represent roughly the constituents of the National Association of Evangelicals and the American Council of Christian Churches. (See Page 40.)

The ACCC is a cooperative organization of those fundamentalist groups which Quebedeaux rightly labels "separatist." This is really the remnants of the older Fundamentalism and continues the same militant, uncompromising stance toward all Christians who disagree with them. They are the true sectarians.

In the NAE ambit we have a coalition of Evangelicals including the older conservative Protestant denomina-

---

C. Norman Kraus is professor of religion and director of the Center for Discipleship at Goshen College. His most recent book is *The Authentic Witness* (Eerdmans, 1979).

Evangelicalism
Ideological Umbrellas

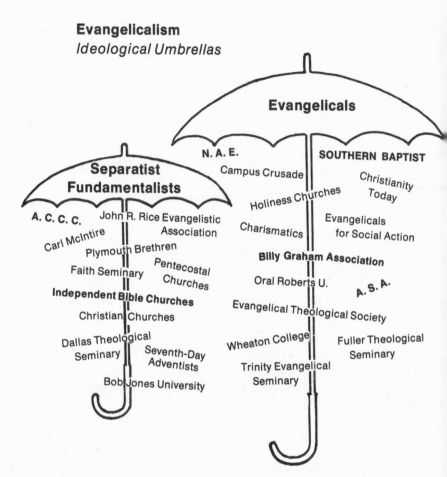

tions; holiness churches like Wesleyan Methodists and Nazarenes; neo-fundamentalist seminaries, colleges, and social action organizations; major evangelistic organizations; charismatic groups; and newly formed radical communal groups. The Southern Baptist Convention with its 12 million plus members and ambitious evangelism ministry does not belong to the NAE, but it is a major force in Evangelicalism.

Used in its broadest sense Evangelicalism would include all these divergent groups. More precisely, however, we should distinguish the two groups, if only because they distinguish between themselves. Many separatist Fundamentalists, for example, are quite unhappy with Billy Graham's tolerant attitudes and easy association with those they consider to be liberal.

Historical Origins of Evangelicalism

American Christianity has always been characterized by plurality. The original settlers from the continent came from a multiplicity of "Christian" nations and brought their own church patterns and beliefs with them. Early attempts at political establishment and uniformity of religion in the colonies soon ran up against the realities of religious pluralism. However, there was concern from the earliest period for the "christianizing" of this new frontier nation, and this required interdenominational cooperation and alliance. After the new federal constitution rejected the legal establishment of a national religion, it became customary for interdenominational alliances and coalitions to form in order to promote religious renewal and moral reform. The pre-Civil War population was predominantly Protestant, and the mood was puritan and pietistic. Thus for many years a loosely knit but highly visible and dominant alliance of evangelical Protestant forces constituted a virtual establishment of religion in American society. Against this background it becomes obvious that the current evangelical coalition is nothing new.

The revival movement was an important component of this Protestant alliance. Prior to the Civil War revivalism put together a coalition of evangelical forces that has, in fact, become a characteristic feature of American church life. It emerged from the frontier camp meeting in the 1830s and became a large urban, nondenominational organization waging campaigns for evangelism, religious renewal, and social reform.

Revivals of religious conviction and fervor began in America as "awakenings" under the aegis of charismatic leaders. Men like Jonathan Edwards and others lit fires of renewal in their own congregations and in addition itinerated to other congregations. The eighteenth-century father of interdenominational revivalism, however, was the Methodist, George Whitefield. He itinerated from Georgia to New England preaching in the open to large crowds who gathered to hear his spellbinding oratory. Later, in the early part of the nineteenth century, under the leadership of Charles Finney and other lesser lights revivalism was born as a nondenominational movement. (Finney wrote the first book on how to have a revival.) When the initial enthusiasm and fervor for revival subsided, the organization did not disband but instead became institutionalized. This institutionalization process is particularly evident after the Civil War beginning with Dwight L. Moody. Moody himself collected great sums of money which he used to found schools and various other religious and social service institutions which continued his legacy. While there was no direct transfer of his revival organization, men like R. A. Torrey, who came to prominence in the administration of his Bible Institute, continued his revivalistic work.

It is probably not too much to say that revivalism continued to carry the fundamentalist movement during the years of its national eclipse, and a renewed and highly organized revivalism has served in the recent decades as a catalyst for the formation of the contemporary Evangelical movement. In fact, the Graham organization, which by this time is a multimillion dollar business, has many characteristics of a new interdenominational denomination and it is far larger and more influential than most present-day denominations.

Perhaps a glance at the accompanying historical chart on page 44 will be helpful in tracing the roots of the contemporary Evangelical movement.

Two theological traditions lie back of the revivalist coalition: American Puritanism which was the bearer of orthodox Calvinism, and Wesleyan holiness which was Arminian in its theology. In the decades following 1730 New England Puritanism was jolted by the religious awakening which focused new attention on the necessity of a conversion *experience* and eventuated in the stirring revivalistic preaching of the "hot gospelers" in Presbyterian circles. But it retained its orthodox Calvinistic base which insisted on unconditional election and justification by faith only.

The Wesleyan emphasis was on individual decision, spiritual self-discipline, and Christian perfection through an experience of entire sanctification.

These two traditions are clearly merged in the revivalism of Charles G. Finney. Finney was a member of the Congregationalist Church (Puritan) and did his theological apprenticeship with a Congregational clergyman. But he had a powerful Wesleyan type conversion which colored all he wrote and did. He preached that salvation is a supernatural work, but that the individual must appropriate it. And he clearly enunciated the means by which a decision for Christ could be induced.

The Evangelical Family Tree

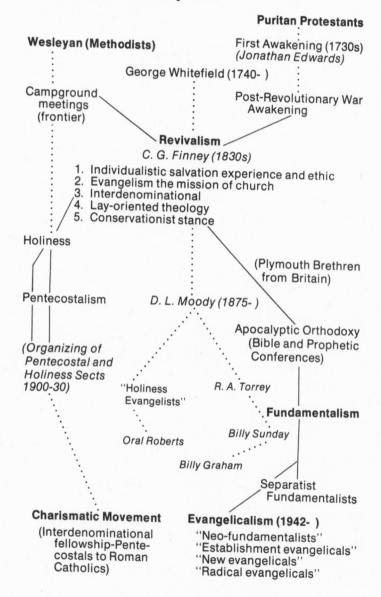

Puritan Protestants

Wesleyan (Methodists)

First Awakening (1730s)
(Jonathan Edwards)

George Whitefield (1740-)

Campground
meetings
(frontier)

Post-Revolutionary War
Awakening

Revivalism

C. G. Finney (1830s)

1. Individualistic salvation experience and ethic
2. Evangelism the mission of church
3. Interdenominational
4. Lay-oriented theology
5. Conservationist stance

Holiness

(Plymouth Brethren
from Britain)

Pentecostalism

D. L. Moody (1875-)

*(Organizing of
Pentecostal and
Holiness Sects
1900-30)*

Apocalyptic Orthodoxy
(Bible and Prophetic
Conferences)

"Holiness
Evangelists"

R. A. Torrey

Fundamentalism

Billy Sunday

Oral Roberts

Billy Graham

Separatist
Fundamentalists

Charismatic Movement

(Interdenominational
fellowship-Pente-
costals to Roman
Catholics)

Evangelicalism (1942-)

"Neo-fundamentalists"
"Establishment evangelicals"
"New evangelicals"
"Radical evangelicals"

His theology was evangelical Arminianism.

Revivalism under his tutelage developed characteristics which distinguish it to the present. First, it focused attention on the *individual's* experience of conversion and accompanying assurance of salvation rather than the life of the individual in the body of Christ. Its ethical precepts likewise aimed at individual sanctification rather than life in its economic, social, and political relationships.

Second, it portrayed evangelism as the primary concern of the church by virtually equating the revival campaign with the mission of the church. Finney's work implicitly began this shift of emphasis, but it became increasingly explicit and prevalent in the era of Moody and early twentieth-century revivalism.

Third, revivalism greatly strengthened and encouraged interdenominational cooperation among the churches. Differences were minimized in favor of the common concern for saving souls. A common evangelical theological base was assumed in the movement. And fourth, the content of that theological base tended to be reduced to the lowest common denominator. The content of revival preaching was increasingly tailored to a lay audience and fashioned to serve the ends of evangelism, namely, to induce decisions for Christ. This not only tended to simplify the theological language in a good sense, but also to reduce inherently complex concepts to clichés and simplistic explanations which could serve the evangelistic purpose.

Last, revivalism was inherently conservative. It assumed that an idealized past experience and orthodoxies provide the Edenic model for the present, and that what is needed is *re*newal, *re*vival, and *re*turn to what has been lost. It fostered the "old-time religion," and without intending to it fostered a kind of nostalgia and backward look rather than confrontation with the real present and future.

During the nineteenth century revivalism clearly divided into two camps along the lines of the pre-Finney period. On the one side was the holiness tradition: associations, camp meetings, and other holiness evangelistic agencies. On the other side was the continuation of Calvinistic or Reformed orthodoxy following the earlier patterns of the revivalists in the Baptist, Congregational, and Presbyterian traditions. This latter group was given new impetus by the impact of Plymouth Brethren teachers who came to the United States after the Civil War. The Plymouth Brethren adhered to a strict Calvinism which was also highly individualistic. According to their teaching the denominational churches were apostate, and the call of the evangelist was for the individual to undergo a spiritual new birth through acceptance of the gospel truth and to "come out" from the apostasy. This, they taught, is the dispensation of the Spirit at work in the hearts of those individuals who have been chosen. The social aspects of salvation implicit in the kingdom of God are deferred to the future millennium.

Both of these traditions have found an identity under the umbrella of contemporary Evangelicalism. We need now to take a closer look at these two evangelical, revivalist-oriented traditions.

The Holiness Tradition

The holiness tradition stems from John Wesley and the early Methodist movement. Wesley taught that "Christian perfection," sometimes also called entire sanctification, is attainable in this life and that Christians should earnestly seek for it. This was a new position in Protestantism. The following chart will help to explain the differences:

Concepts of Sanctification

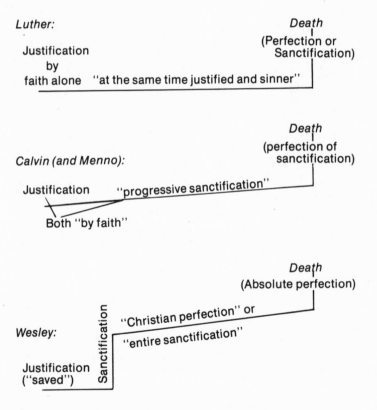

Luther:

Justification
by
faith alone   "at the same time justified and sinner"

Death
(Perfection or Sanctification)

Calvin (and Menno):

Justification   "progressive sanctification"

Both "by faith"

Death
(perfection of sanctification)

Wesley:

Justification
("saved")

Sanctification

"Christian perfection" or
"entire sanctification"

Death
(Absolute perfection)

Luther had taught that justification is by faith alone, and that the Christian's righteousness is an "alien righteousness" imputed in Christ. We might characterize his position as teaching that Christians live a life of continual justification. They remain at the same time "justified and sinners." Perfection or sanctification will come only with death, and the freedom from this body.

John Calvin also stressed salvation by grace through faith, but he taught the possibility of a progressive sanctification. Holiness is not through any self-effort or works righteousness. Our righteousness is always faith righteousness, and "traces of our imperfection remain to give us occasion for humility." Nevertheless, a genuine growth in Christ is possible for the true believer. Perfection comes only with death. This, I might add, was essentially Menno Simons view also.

John Wesley introduced the concept of justification and sanctification as a double work of grace. Justification initiates the experience and santification perfects it. Christians may be perfect in love and intention, but he said that such perfection is *relative*—a quite contradictory concept! Even after the instantaneous experience of entire sanctification one can continue to grow in Christian holiness. (The inclining line on the chart following the sanctification indicates such growth.) Wesley did not speak of sinless perfection. Such absolute purity comes only after death.

Such teaching was introduced into America by Methodist preachers already prior to the Revolutionary War, but the self-conscious development of holiness churches is a much later matter. After the Civil War the National Holiness Association was formed (1867) for the purpose of promoting Christian holiness or entire sanctification. The Association organized camp meetings, published lists of "holiness evangelists," encouraged the establishments of missions called "soul-saving stations," and published holiness periodicals.

While the movement was dominated by Methodists in the early years, it was interdenominational and gradually was pushed to the periphery of the Methodist denomination. It became increasingly identified with the broader revivalist movement, but continued its own special emphases such as personal moral discipline and separation from the world. There was strong preaching against the worldliness of jewelry, neckties, use of tobacco and alcohol, and frivolous entertainment. Abstinence from these things was a mark of holiness.

The work of the NHA was at first interdenominational, but in the 1880s some leaders began to preach "come-outism," and groups associated with it began to split off and form independent holiness churches. Then in 1894 at its General Conference the Methodist Church (South) began to publicly disavow the holiness emphasis. From this time new schisms developed such as the Nazarenes, and Pilgrim Holiness.[1]

During this period (1880-1910) the "come-outers" were aggressive and critical of traditional denominations. They were quite ready to proselyte, and they made inroads into the Mennonite and Friends churches as well as others. In the 1890s trouble developed among Mennonite churches of Missouri, Kansas, and Iowa where the movement was strong. In 1898 a schism occurred among the Berne Mennonites and the Missionary Church Association was formed. They were especially critical of the conservative churches which preached "once saved, always saved" doctrine and hung the entire Christian experience upon an initial acceptance of Jesus Christ as Savior.

Emergence of Pentecostalism

Pentecostalism emerged as a further modification of
the holiness teaching. We can date this from the beginning of the "Fire-Baptized Holiness Church" in Iowa,
1895. This radical group founded by B. H. Irwin taught
that the sanctified Christians should seek to enter into
the full dispensation of the Spirit by a "baptism of the
Holy Spirit and fire."[2] This was referred to as a pentecostal baptism beyond the second work of sanctification.
In 1901 Charles Parham of Kansas, who is generally
recognized as the first organizer of the Pentecostal movement, had a similar pentecostal experience of a baptism
of *power*.[3]

Without pursuing the history of the movement, one
can outline how the Pentecostal movement modified the
teaching of Wesleyan sanctification. First, it added a
third baptism of power or filling, which was identified
with the Pentecost experience, to the work of sanctification. In some cases this was theologically underscored
with the language of dispensationalism as a spiritual con-
sumation to be expected in the *dispensation of the Spirit*.
The *sign* of this third work was speaking in tongues,
which in the first instances were identified with actual
foreign languages.

Gradually in many parts of the movement the element
of sanctification became muted and the baptism or filling
was simply associated with the Pentecostal experience of
tongues which was to be sought by works of faith—full
repentance and total surrender, prayer and appropriation
of Christ.[4] Emphasis shifted from the ethical holiness and
social concern to individual extra-rational (emotional) religious experience with great stress on the "supernatural" character of the experience. Clear distinction

Pentecostal-Holiness

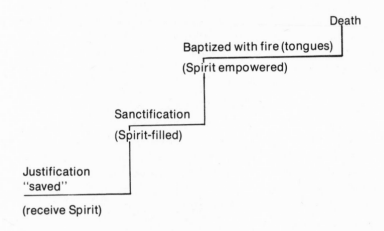

Pentecostal (Charismatic)

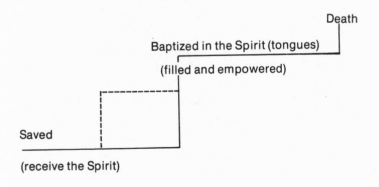

was made between the sign of tongues which every Spirit-baptized person receives and the gift of tongues which some continue to have. And other spiritual gifts such as prophecy, wisdom, knowledge, and healing were also sought and experienced.

Finally, it was taught that physical as well as spiritual healing is included in the atonement. Spirit-baptized people should expect and pray for healing and use medical resources only as a last resort. With this the way was prepared for the wedding of mass revivalism and healing campaigns with which we have become familiar.

During the early 1900s many of the miniscule Pentecostal sects merged to form larger denominations like the Assemblies of God and the Pentecostal Holiness Church, but the movement remained separatist and sectarian into the 1960s. It continued to grow in numbers both in this country and abroad, especially in South America where it became the first major Protestant challenge to Roman Catholicism. Then with the impact of the charismatic movement Pentecostalism itself began to open up to ecumenical fellowship.

Charismatics or Neo-pentecostals

In the late 1950s stories about a new religious phenomenon in the traditional denominations began breaking in the news media. *Time* entitled one such news release "Blue Tongues at Yale." Then there was word that Peter Marshall, Jr., and a group of some fifty student colleagues were experiencing glossolalia at Princeton Theological Seminary. Simultaneously there were reports of healing services in Episcopal, Lutheran, and Presbyterian churches. Somewhat later, after Vatican Council II, the Roman Catholics were having similar *charismata* displayed among them. The movement spread rapidly in most denominations including the Mennonites.

Again, our purpose is not to tell the history but to describe some of its significant characteristics. It is Pentecostal with a new spirit and significant modifications of traditional Pentecostal theology.

Perhaps the most distinctive and attractive characteristic of the new movement is its emphasis on the unity of the Spirit and grassroots ecumenical fellowship. It has decisively rejected the "come-outism" and sectarian spirit of classical Pentecostalism. It is of interest to note by the way that this was the initial emphasis of the holiness associations in the period 1830-1870.

Along with this ecumenical spirit the movement stresses the renewal of the whole panoply of spiritual gifts to the church for its life and mission. There is strong insistence upon the coming of the Holy Spirit as a *continuing event* in the church. The individual experience is one of "release in the Spirit," enablement, and a new sense of the reality of faith. The gift of tongues is viewed as highly desirable, but not as the only and necessary sign of the baptism of the Spirit.

As the charismatic and pentecostal traditions have intermingled some Pentecostal doctrines have permeated the movement, but in its more pristine form the charismatic movement has rejected some of the more questionable definitions and doctrines of traditional Pentecostalism. The older notion that tongues are a miraculous gift of human language has been discarded. The experience is viewed rather as an exercise in ecstatic prayer and praise—a speaking to God. The teaching that physical healing is included in the atonement and Spirit-baptized believers should expect to receive miraculous healing as part of their salvation has been dropped. And last, the movement puts no emphasis on entire sanctifica-

tion, however there is insistence that the "fruit of the
Spirit" should accompany the "gifts of the Spirit."

The Fundamentalist Tradition

The second tradition that informs contemporary Evangelicalism is Fundamentalism. Indeed, its *post*-Funda-
mentalist character is one of its most distinctive features.

The term Fundamentalist is often used to include all
sorts of doctrinally conservative sectarian groups including the Pentecostals. I intend to use it in a more
restricted sense. It is true that during the period of controversy between Fundamentalism and Liberalism the
Pentecostals imbided a fundamentalistic spirit and by
and large adopted dispensationalist eschatology. But
deep, recognized differences persisted between them
and those Fundamentalists who traced their lineage from
John Calvin.

Fundamentalism is self-consciously Calvinistic (Reformed) in its theological tenets and assumptions. I have
shown in my *Dispensationalism in America* (John Knox,
1958) that the leaders of the Bible and Prophetic
Conference movements in the late 1800s were predominantly Calvinistic in their theological and church
affiliations. The new apocalyptic version of orthodoxy introduced into this country by the Darbyites, or Plymouth
Brethren, actually exaggerated Calvinistic doctrines in
some respects.

Fundamentalism's concern was not primarily church
renewal as such, but rather the maintenance of the conservative Puritan (Calvinistic) religious ethos of America
as a Christian nation. It emerged at a time when the conservative Protestant base of American society was
seriously threatened by new social and intellectual

forces. The traditional patterns of revivalism and denominational orthodoxies could not or would not stem the tide of Darwinism, scientism, liberal theology, biblical criticism, Roman Catholicism, and sectarian movements such as Christian Science and Pentecostalism. Thus a new religious coalition formed across denominational lines to keep America Christian in the orthodox, Puritan sense of that word.

I think it might be argued that what has traditionally held the Evangelical movement together is an emphasis upon the supernatural experience of salvation by grace rather than a given set of fundamental doctrinal propositions. Prior to the period of fundamentalist dominance within conservative Protestantism evangelical doctrine in its Arminian, Calvinist, and Lutheran variations could be assumed as a working interdenominational basis. Unitarianism was a minority heresy, and "infidelity" was an external foe. The burning question had to do with the nature and theological presuppositions of the Christian's experience. With the emergence of modern Liberalism in the churches, the supernatural new birth became one of the fundamental *doctrines*. Emphasis shifted to correct doctrinal statements and an objectified authority for truth found in an inerrant Bible.

Fundamentalism's primary interest was theological. Its strategy was to focus on simplified formulations of essential or fundamental doctrines, from which it derives its name. Already in 1878 the new movement, which I have called apocalyptic orthodoxy, self-consciously initiated an aggressive attack on the new intellectual enemies of orthodox Christianity. They attacked evolution, rationalistic criticism of the Bible, socialism, humanistic views of Christ and atonement, and humanitarian

reform posturing as Christianity. They expressed great
alarm at "infidelity in the pulpit," which, they said, was
already undermining the churches. Thus their
theological statements were defensive and polemic in
posture. They were worded in sharply antithetical,
defiant terms which implied opposition and contrast.
And they tended to be stated in stark unqualified and
often oversimplified terms.

Fundamentalism viewed the Bible as the intellectual
source book for theological data which it used to form a
system of definitions and doctrines. Then in turn it
equated its fundamental definitions, which were extra-
polated from Scripture, with the Scripture message itself.
Clichés and catchwords became the criteria for orthodoxy. For example, how one referred to Jesus could
indicate the degree of a person's orthodoxy. The fully
fundamental designation was the "Lord Jesus Christ."
Those who used only Jesus were suspected of liberalism.
The only sound and effective theory of atonement was
the "penal substitutionary blood atonement." "Vicarious
sacrifice" was considered inadequate for sound theology.
To be fully and consistently orthodox one had to hold to
the literal premillennial second coming of Christ.
Nonmillennialists became suspect.

In order to guarantee the Bible as an infallibly
trustworthy source for theology they insisted on the
theory of verbal plenary inspiration and inerrancy of the
text. While they stated explicitly that they did not hold to
a literal dictation theory, they said just as clearly that the
result was the same as if it had been literally dictated.
Their logic demanded a letter-perfect book. Both in
seventeenth-century Orthodoxy and later Fundamentalism inspiration was attributed to syllables and letters

as well as words. In its refined form this applied only to the original writings, but in practice it carried over to the King James text. The authority of its literal text was considered absolute on every subject it touched.

While Fundamentalism put much stress on being "born again" it defined it as a private and spiritual experience. This was conversion as theological justification rather than a moral reorientation. Such an understanding presupposed a strict Calvinistic view of mankind's total depravity, that is, total inability to effect any spiritual change in one's life, and upon a concept of faith as belief in correct doctrine.

Attention focused on the individual rather than the saved community. By the beginning of the twentieth century Darbyite pessimism about the institutional church as "apostate Christendom" had pretty well carried the day. The true church was seen as a spiritual fellowship of individual Christians joined in a network of independent "come-outer" congregations, Bible schools, and evangelistic organizations of one kind or another. There was little or no social action other than continued emphasis on temperance; and social service programs such as the Mennonite Central Committee were suspect as "social gospel" programs. By the 1920s there was little expectation that there would be any significant societal change for the better, and Christ's return was expected imminently. Evangelism was a matter of gathering out the elect and preparing the way for the cataclysmic second coming of Christ.

Two Traditions Converge

One of the symbolic events of the late 1960s was the personal meeting of Billy Graham and Oral Roberts, representatives of the two major traditions in Evangelicalism. By the time of the meeting Roberts had moved away from some of his more extreme Pentecostal emphases, but nevertheless the meeting seemed to signal the acceptance of his ministry by evangelicals. Separatist fundamentalists and neo-fundamentalists of the Campus Crusade variety, of course, have not acknowledged the validity of the Holiness-Pentecostal doctrine of a Spirit baptism, but the moderate voices of the two camps seem to have called a truce although distinct alignments and programs continue.

The following comparative chart summarizes the distinctive characteristics of the two movements:

Distinguishing Characteristics of Holiness-Pentecostal and Fundamentalist Movements

HOLINESS-PENTECOSTAL (charismatic)	FUNDAMENTALIST (didactic)
Wesleyan (Arminian) *Spirit:* gifts and manifestations of the Spirit give evidence of authentic Christian life.	Calvinistic *Bible:* the words of an inerrant Bible give the assurance of salvation.
Experience centered: emphasizes vital relation to Spirit and continuing "miracles" in life of Christians	*Theology centered:* emphasizes correct belief, faith not feeling or miracles is proper sphere for Christian living.
Extra - or nonrational elements of gospel recognized.	*Rational* and logically consistent message of the gospel of salvation stressed.
Church as congregation/community is center for nurture and fellowship.	*Church is nondenominational* spiritual fellowship and evangelistic agent.
Sectarian ideal—separation of church and nation	*Nonsectarian ideal*—"Christian nation" with church legally separate but influential in public life.

| "*Holiness*" ethic of sanctification and "separation from the world." | "*Born-again*" ethic of individual justification in the midst of the world. |

A major continuing difference between the Holiness-Pentecostal tradition and Fundamentalism, old and new, lies in the Holiness-Pentecostal insistence on a normative experience of the Spirit's presence in addition to conversion. Two facets of this must be underscored: first, that there is a normal experience of the Holy Spirit *subsequent* to the new birth; and second, that this is an identifiable *experience* which leads to a direct awareness of the indwelling of the Spirit.

Fundamentalists stress faith/belief rather than experience. They have been extremely suspicious of feelings, which they identify with "experience," as a spiritual indicator, and they insist that assurance of salvation is based *only* on belief in the Scripture's promises. Theologically they fear a compromise with a new works righteousness. Although they may agree to subsequent growth in understanding and commitment, they do not subscribe to a normativeness of a "second blessing."

Finally, a divergence in the concept of the church seems to have been bridged in part from both sides but remains a relative difference in emphasis. The Holiness-Pentecostal tradition has been sectarian in church life and ethic while the fundamentalist tradition has been spiritualist and nonsectarian. Fundamentalism has stressed a nondenominational fellowship of individual Christians who have been born again. There is virtually no emphasis on the community of believers. By default if not by overt teaching the "Christian nation" remains the implicit Fundamentalist ideal. Born-again Christians work as individuals within the nation accepting its basic social and economic values and systems. Following the guidelines of an earlier pietistic orthodoxy it calls for individual morality and spiritual separation from evils in the world, but such evils are not defined in terms of systemic social injustice. Fundamentalism has been extremely slow to challenge public moral or social practice in the name of Christ. Indeed, born-again Christians have been the backbone of individualistic capitalism with its inequalities and racial discrimination.

During the decades 1935-55 when Fundamentalism was eclipsed by a more dominant middle of the road Protestant Liberalism, it retrenched into a nonpolitical, spiritualist position that put all its emphasis on individual salvation. Now that it has again gained significance as a religious movement it has also reemerged as a political force seeking to regulate morals and public religious practice by law. As in the past it has made alliance with conservative nationalistic political, military, and economic forces to bolster an aggressive America first policy.

The holiness movement from the time of Wesley himself has been much more socially conscious. The Wesleyan Methodists broke with the larger denomination over the issue of slavery in 1843. The Finney revivals led to concern for social reform. And although Pentecostalism was heavily influenced by fundamentalistic doctrine and ethics in the period from 1910 to the present, even so it remained more sensitive to public moral issues. For example, it has a more nondiscriminatory record on the race issue.

The holiness movement has been far more consistently sectarian in the precise sociological meaning of that word. It has had a clearer sense of the church as a community separate from the worldly social order, and it has required a personal and social (not political) ethic consistent with such separation. Its holiness ethic has given it a sensitivity to broader social issues. This concern with community and obedience to Christ in the social areas of life has found renewed focus in the charismatic movement.

One of the most hopeful signs within Evangelicalism is the convergence of the radical Evangelicals and the charismatic communities. This coalition and the impact of third world theologies may be the hope of a renewal of authentic Christian witness in the Western world.

CHAPTER 4

Evangelicalism and Radical Discipleship

Wes Michaelson

I was raised an Evangelical. My decision for Christ was made after hearing about Jesus coming into my heart at the age of four. In junior high I couldn't take a class in social dancing with all my friends. In high school I used to wonder whether I should carry my Bible on top of my other books as a witness. A more personally enriching experience of faith came through a Young Life club. My adolescent rebellion consisted of choosing not to go to Wheaton College.

The Evangelical tradition gave me my faith and nurtured my commitment to Christ as Lord. But as I sought to relate the gospel to political and social realities I sensed the deep failures of the modern Evangelical tradition. Thousands of others from this tradition have gone on the same pilgrimage I did then.

During the past decade, these failures were exhibited most blatantly around the war in Indochina. Countless

---

Wes Michaelson, a member of the Sojourners Community in Washington, D.C., is associate editor of *Sojourners*. He was formerly an administrative assistant to Senator Mark Hatfield.

sons and daughters of strong evangelical homes could never understand the complicity of the Evangelicals in what was so manifestly cruel. Most Evangelicals blessed the charge, sanctified the bombs, and damned those who refused to participate. The handful of born-again dissenters was hardly tolerated and nearly ostracized from fellowship.

Theologically, Evangelicals have abandoned the biblical hope that the kingdom of God breaks into our history, here and now. As one Evangelical leader confessed, the kingdom of God is about as natural a part of Evangelicals' conversation as one of those strange names in a Dostoevski novel. There has been little belief in the kingdom of God as a coming political and social reality to which the church is now to be a sign.

Cutting away the kingdom of God from the message of Jesus, the Evangelical tradition has proclaimed a politically neutral gospel, separating things spiritual from things political. While this separation has broken down in practice—Evangelicalism in this century has actually bolstered conservative political forces—it has been maintained in theory. This amputated gospel has enabled Evangelicals to place troubling political questions like the Vietnam war, the division between wealth and poverty, the nuclear arms race, and the civil rights movement outside the province of Jesus' word. Convictions about political questions have been regarded as matters of personal preference, like a favorite color for shirts or which football team to root for. No crucial interdependence between political convictions and faith in Christ has been admitted. (The exceptions, of course, are those overt attempts to ordain right-wing politics with biblical justification.)

The shortcomings of the Evangelical heritage, however, have not just been political and social; Evangelicalism has been inadequate to provide the long-term spiritual nurture essential to discipleship. Evangelical spirituality has frequently been equated with the emotions coming in the wake of a born-again experience. But after six months, a year, or a decade—when the quiet time and the close walk with Jesus stop radiating the same warmth they did in the afterglow of conversion— one is frequently left feeling guilty, isolated, and not knowing exactly where to turn.

Because Evangelical spirituality has been so highly individualistic, there usually has been little experience of the church as a community. What communal sense there is has resulted more from a legalistic separation from the outside world than from the reality of koinonia as it is described in the New Testament. Most Evangelical worship has been designed to bolster personal piety rather than to nurture the corporate life of Christ's body.

Contemporary Evangelicalism shows some signs of change at each of these points. New sensitivities to the imperatives of biblical justice can be found, as well as a growth of interest in deeper expressions of fellowship.

There are those, sometimes called radical Evangelicals, who are attempting to redeem the Evangelical heritage and to forge it into a movement bearing witness to radical discipleship. They are attempting to recover the best of the tradition built around the proclamation that Jesus is Lord. That conviction, after all, is central to Evangelicalism. Further, they share the Evangelical commitment to biblical authority for life and witness. Their concern has increasingly focused, however, on the biblical teaching about social or community implications of the gospel while in no way denying the individual and personal aspects. In the wake of Watergate and Vietnam, most Evangelicals now admit that faith in Christ does have some relevance to questions of social and political justice. That is a decisive, major change.

Concern for social justice is part of the earlier heritage of Evangelicalism, and it is very helpful in awakening Evangelicals to the imperatives of biblical justice to be able to demonstrate that this is within their own tradition. The problem is that one must go back pretty far to find it. In this century the movement has strongly reacted to any version of the gospel which emphasizes the historical meaning of the kingdom of God. In all honesty one has to admit that the heritage, at least in this century, is one of dominant individualism. Its great, almost sole emphasis has been on converting or saving the soul. Questions of discipleship, justice, and the shape of the church were invariably relegated to secondary or peripheral status. One cannot ignore these realities. At best the historical picture is mixed.

There is a further problem in trying to draw exclusively upon contemporary Evangelicalism for the forming of a movement of radical discipleship today. That problem has to do with the present social and psychological status of Evangelicals in our nation. In the past Evangelicals considered themselves to be an overlooked minority group who nevertheless carried the heart of the American nation in their souls. Now since the Carter candidacy the secular media has paid remarkable attention to the movement. Evangelicals have been discovered, and that has finally given them the long-awaited cultural acceptance. Tired of being ignored and ridiculed, Evangelicals now bask in the limelight of their

new popularity. Indeed, they seem all too willing to be
seduced by their culture.

Their weakness to resist the temptation of cultural
assimilation stems from two sources. First, their former
ethical and theological position of separation from the
world characteristically ignored the most basic conflicts
between the gospel and American culture. Separation
applied only in comparatively small matters of personal
ethics. Now in their newly attained acceptance they are
quite vulnerable. They have legitimately rejected the
older, narrow, more legalistic morality, but they have no
other theological or ethical tradition to fall back on for
guidance. Consequently in far too many instances they
are simply accepting the culture on its own terms.

And their sudden social acceptance and even popularity exacerbates the problem. After being neglected for
so long, Evangelicals are eager to prove that they can
make it in this society. Indeed, many of them are making
it on the terms that our society understands the best: success, fame, prosperity, and social influence. But such success unavoidably involves them in a certain accommodation to the sociopolitical system. In order to succeed they
must demonstrate a thoroughgoing, uncritical loyalty to
the American way of life and a fidelity to the American
system of economics and politics. So now that they have
finally been discovered, Evangelicals are all too ready to
be enticed into the cultural mainstream.

Nor is this new Evangelical embrace of the American
culture to be identified simply with the old right-wing
Fundamentalist stance. It comes in a more subtle guise,
namely, that success, acceptability, and respect in our society should come naturally to anyone who is "born
again," and that in fact conversion ought to produce

these fruits. The message that the media-centered Evangelical revival most clearly conveys to the larger society is that being born again is a very highly personalized experience which brings inner peace and healing. Those elements of the gospel which are least marketable, for example, self-sacrifice, servanthood, the way of the cross, identification with the poor and oppressed, and a prophetic witness for justice and peace, simply do not get communicated in the media approach. And this is not just a limitation or perversion of the media. What the media observes and reports is in large measure correct. At the heart of the matter is a hunger for legitimacy—a legitimacy which Evangelicals are defining in terms of the present system. The question whether this present system is legitimate in biblical terms is simply not being asked. Therefore the popularity of Evangelicalism has become one of the basic impediments to its recovering the tradition of radical discipleship.

What Nurtures Radical Evangelicalism?

For the above reasons many of those who have emerged from the Evangelical tradition toward a more biblically radical understanding of the gospel are looking to other sources and movements in the Christian church for the nurturing of their faith. The major sources of inspiration and guidance are the Anabaptists, the Charismatics, Third World Christians stressing social justice, and contemporary Roman Catholic contemplatives like Thomas Merton.

1. *The Anabaptists.* As a theological and communal tradition, Anabaptism has provided a unique point of identification for many from an evangelical heritage who are taking the call to discipleship seriously in our time.

This is because of the pivotal questions which, historically, Anabaptism has asked and attempted to answer:

What does it mean to give our lives according to all the demands of the gospel?

How can our lives be molded consistently by the pattern of Christ's servanthood?

What are the concrete implications of loving our enemies?

How is the church to live out its life as a called community of God's people?

The evangelical tradition has generally evaded these questions; only in the last few years have such concerns even entered evangelical discourse. Anabaptism has urgently asked those questions for centuries.

When younger evangelicals, appalled by their churches' support for the Vietnam war, began challenging Evangelicalism's conformity to American culture, they started asking, quite independently, the same theological questions which Mennonites and other Anabaptists had asked centuries ago.

The discovery of the Anabaptist tradition by these radicalized Evangelicals had a humbling and encouraging effect, convincing them that their questions were not unique to this generation. This discovery was a clear sign that the task was not to construct a theology which was merely a reaction to the Vietnam war, but rather to probe biblically for what was always true about the gospel.

Any tradition brings with it its own baggage. Its original impulses are likely to be misinterpreted and diluted by later generations. Certainly this is true of the Anabaptist/Mennonite heritage.

Often that heritage has provided a rationale for a

retreat from the world, rather than the impetus for the
church to give its life on behalf of the world. The ever-
present danger in such forms of sectarian withdrawal is
that the boundaries of God's kingdom become defined in
extremely parochial and self-justifying ways. Those
tendencies, however, should not obscure the biblically
rooted understanding of discipleship which the Anabaptist tradition offers to the church.

2. *The Charismatics*. When many of us began grasp-
ing the social, political, and economic meaning of the
gospel, we assumed that the charismatic renewal movement was about the last place to turn for nuture and en-
couragement. Since that movement demonstrated little if
any openness toward the prophetic dimensions of the
gospel—it was a largely reactionary social and political
force in society—this mistrust was understandable.

But as we understood the starting point for the witness
to God's kingdom to be the creation of a faithful people,
we began tentatively exploring certain segments of the
charismatic movement receptive to the political claims of
the gospel. That testing has now matured into bonds of
trust, nurture, and mutual edification.

The charismatic movement can bring to radical discipleship a deep experience of what it means for the church
to be a community, functioning concretely as a dynamic
alternative social and spiritual environment. Seasoned
charismatics are not obsessed with individualistic gifts;
rather, their focus is on the calling of a people, corporately, to be the full expression of Christ's body.

Some groups within the charismatic renewal have
been moving toward radical political and social understandings of the gospel. In my judgment, this movement
is a crucial event in contemporary church history. When-

ever a charismatically influenced fellowship comes to grasp the meaning of its new life as existing not in and for itself, but for the sake of God's purposes of justice in the world, then it often embraces acts of prophetic witness in an unhesitant and graceful manner.

While major currents of the charismatic movement remain closed to such witness, sweeping stereotypes can no longer be applied to the whole charismatic renewal movement. Many whose Christian radicalism once separated them from charismatics now have found some among them to be a wellspring of nurture. Those charismatics have helped put flesh on the vision of a biblically radical gospel by spiritually supporting growing fellowships of such believers.

3. *The Social Justice Activists.* Central to any understanding of faithful discipleship is the biblical imperative to seek fundamental social justice, motivated by God's compassion for those who are impoverished and afflicted. Certain Christians have witnessed to these truths with a compelling clarity and constancy, and they are nurturing all those who have discovered that conversion to Christ includes a commitment to solidarity with the poor.

Third World Christians like Brazilian Archbishop Dom Helder Camara, many black Christians, other voices of prophetic social justice in the American church, liberation theologians, and those who are attempting to integrate their faith with socialism and the insights of Marxism all share a commitment to economic and social justice. These believers know that justice lies at the heart of God's intention for the world, that the Bible gives revolutionary hope to the poor and the oppressed, and that the biblical message condemns the established structures of power and injustice.

Those who have emerged from evangelical back-grounds to a faith which refuses to segregate personal conversion and social activism find a sense of rapport with these Christians. From them we hear clear words of judgment about the American economic order and its worldwide dominion over people's lives—words which are prompted by the biblical message, but which have been foreign to evangelical conversation.

It is ironic that many of us feel greater ease in fellow-ship with Christians whose commitment to justice is steadfast, despite other theological disagreements, than with many Evangelicals. With Evangelicals we still experience significant differences over the concrete meaning of Christ's lordship.

We have critical questions to ask many of these Chris-tian social activists, however. First, what is the relation-ship of faith to ideology? Liberation theology rightly ac-cuses the American church of letting its theology be cap-tivated by capitalism. But is the only possible response a theology which runs a risk of being captivated by a Marxist ideology?

Second, can the use of violence, even in the most just causes of liberation, ever be reconciled with the biblical witness of Christ's commandments?

Third, what is the role of the church in the process of fundamental social and political change? Does the Chris-tian look to secular movements of history as the exclusive source of such change, or is the starting point God's ac-tion in calling a faithful people to be Christ's body? In other words, does the agenda begin with political reform or revolution (depending on whether one is liberal or radical), or does it begin with forming a people to follow God's purposes in history?

The evangelical tradition remains in desperate need of those streams of the church which flow from the biblical truth that God is with the oppressed, and that God's intention is liberation. The question of how this is to be made historically concrete can be addressed only after we come to a consensus about God's purposes of justice and liberation for all humanity.

4. *The Contemplatives and the Catholic Left.* There are two tributaries in the Catholic tradition which uniquely feed those called to a radical gospel. The first is the Catholic left, represented in Dorothy Day and the Catholic Worker movement. For decades their faith has propelled them to share their life with the destitute, joining the cause of oppressed workers, and struggling to implement a vision of radical social change. The Catholic Worker has felt most at home with their Lord in soup kitchens. Unlike many of their fellow Catholics, they harbor a healthy skepticism about the way social and political power is arranged. Theirs has been a voice of biblically rooted dissent. It is dissent which bears the stamp of authenticity in living with the poor and for them.

Throughout the Catholic left, from social reformers like Michael Harrington to prophetic dissenters like Dan Berrigan, a common debt is owed to the Catholic Worker movement. Increasingly, this same debt is acknowledged by many of us whose tradition has been evangelical rather than Catholic, but who have seen the Catholic Worker's identification with the poor a witness to the gospel marked by a simplicity and purity uncommon in our own upbringing.

The other nurturing Catholic contribution is the contemplative and monastic tradition of the church. The monastic movement has always professed that seeking the purity of the gospel in our lives requires (to use an old Catholic term) spiritual formation.

Whenever discipleship has been deepened in the history of the church, it has been accompanied by questions like, "How are we matured spiritually?" "How are we guided and nurtured, both individually and corporately, in that development?" Concern for radical discipleship today which omits any sensitivity to spiritual formation is a grave mistake; it may be radical, but it will not be a call to full discipleship.

Those emerging from the Evangelical tradition have frequently discovered its inability to spiritually sustain a pilgrimage of faithful discipleship. The danger, however, is that radical political witness will become the substitute for an authentic spirituality, rather than its fruit.

Here the contemplative, monastic tradition has a vital contribution to make. This tradition has the maturity to nourish faith in the midst of darkness—both inward and outward. Through centuries contemplatives have struggled to know the meaning of living as pilgrims in this world, not simply out of a desire to flee it, but because of their thirst to know God, and share in God's life.

Of course, contemplatives can err in replacing an actively prayerful engagement with the world and its pain by a disengaged quest for spiritual ecstasy. But that need not be the case, and is a departure from the distinctly Christian contemplative tradition. It is instructive that Thomas Merton, who secluded himself in the spiritual regimen of a Trappist monastery, was one of the first and most discerning prophetic voices within the church to protest against the war in Indochina.

The most vulnerable point in the contemporary movement toward radical discipleship is the need, and often the lack, of an authentic spirituality, one which can sustain a long and arduous struggle, upbuilding life lived in distinct nonconformity with the culture. That such a struggle is our destiny is beyond any doubt. The question is whether we can be nurtured to embrace that struggle not merely with endurance, but rather with celebration, with worship, and with joy.

This calling necessitates building a vital worship base for our life together as Christ's body. In fact, this renewed life should find its source in such worship.

Both individually and communally, those given to a radical following of Jesus will be unable to continue on their journey of faith without feeding the fundamental desire to know God, to do God's will, and to be molded by this hunger and thirst for righteousness.

The Evangelical heritage asks the question, "Are you saved?" That is a vital question. Yet it is rendered meaningless when it is severed from the questions asked by each of these other streams in the church's life. The Anabaptists ask, "What does it mean to be saved?"; the Charismatics ask, "What does it mean to belong to the body of Christ?"; the social justice activists ask, "What does it mean to preach salvation to the poor?"; and the Catholic contemplatives ask, "What does it mean to live life in God's presence?"

Our journey has led us to ask and answer all these questions together. We have been enriched, in distinct ways, by all these traditions, each of which has begun to feel, in some way, a part of our own spiritual heritage.

Discipleship Issues in Radical Evangelicalism

Radical Evangelicals are characterized by their renewed sensitivity to the social dimensions of the gospel and by their concern to bring a biblically radical critique to bear on contemporary political and social issues. There are a number of such issues which not only have crucial importance for the life of our society and the future of humanity, but which relate directly to the shape of the church. Any movement of authentic discipleship has to confront these issues in our day.

The first is the nuclear arms race. In many respects this transcends all the other issues simply because of its horrifying consequences. It is no exaggeration to say that the nuclear arms confrontation betrays a loss of our corporate sanity. The facts and figures numb the conscience: The U.S. arsenal of 8,500 missles can destroy the Soviet Union not just once but 30 times over, and it can destroy all the globe 12 times. Yet every day we continue to produce the equivalent of three more nuclear weapons. All of these are far more powerful than the bomb we first dropped on Hiroshima.

Beyond that, we refuse to renounce the right to use these weapons of nuclear destruction first in a potential conflict. Most Americans do not realize it is not the *policy* of this country to use these weapons only in retaliation to an attack. Historically we are the first and only nation to have used them. Despite the rhetoric of detente, each day the arms race becomes more deadly. Since the SALT talks began, our own arsenal of nuclear strength has doubled. Although it takes two to race, the truth is that we are the ones who have set the pace. Because of our reliance on the technology of nuclear energy an estimated 35 to 40 nations will be able to possess nuclear weapons by the end of this century, not to mention terrorist groups who may acquire them. That is why some leading scientists and arms control experts are saying that nuclear war is becoming probable, perhaps inevitable, before the year 2000.

Even the most generous versions of classical Christian "just war" theory would condemn the use of nuclear weapons as a terrible national sin. Yet nearly all the Evangelical churches have remained silent on this issue, unable to utter a word. Nuclear war is genocidal. Yet daily we prepare for such a war without a moral qualm, convinced of its necessity and convinced of our own righteousness. Christians must be willing to say "no" to nuclear weapons, not because we are naive about the realities of sin and evil in the world, but rather precisely because we are acutely aware of those realities, and know that they reside not only in our adversaries but in ourselves as well. The church in the name of Christ's lordship and kingdom must renounce such apalling sin. We cannot expect genuine initiatives toward disarmament on the part of the nation when the church itself sanctions such continuing violence!

The second is the discrepency between the world's rich and poor. In a world where resources are finite, the rich nations' monopoly of wealth is the prime (not the only) cause of the poor's plight. Such a statement makes Evangelicals uncomfortable, but it is a commonplace biblical insight. Evangelicals in the best capitalistic American tradition would like to believe that as we get richer the poor have more hope of prospering. That formula may soothe consciences, but it does not concur with the facts. The lifestyle of abundance, consumption, and waste which thoughtlessly dominates our society cannot be reconciled with the imperatives of economic justice.

Few subjects in the Bible are stated with as much

clarity as the warnings against wealth and riches, yet it is hard to imagine a biblical teaching that has been so neglected and ignored by Evangelicals. The first passages that are demythologized are those dealing with the Sermon on the Mount. I find that deeply ironic in a tradition which places so much stress on the Bible being the Word of God.

The third issue is the moral and spiritual validity of our present economic system. That system is grounded on a crass materialism which represents the functioning belief and values of most Americans. Our economic system depends upon and fosters human selfishness. It nurtures greed. One has only to watch the TV advertisements for one evening to see that! It allows for the concentration of wealth, and its goal of maximizing profit is almost always given priority over the meeting of human need. It is difficult to understand why all Christians do not raise basic questions about such a system. As a matter of fact, the tendency of the Evangelical and main-line Protestant churches has been to bless capitalism rather than question it.

Theologically the Evangelical tradition has justified capitalism in the most unique way. We are told that capitalism is wise, good, and morally superior to any other economic system because it recognizes and structures itself around the realities of human sin and selfishness. Thus sin becomes the means of ascribing virtue to this economic order. But such reasoning has its problems. For example, all of us recognize the reality of sexual lust. But does that lead any of us to advocate a system of legalized open prostitution which is justified as being morally sound and desirable? All of us recognize the human tendency to lie, but does that lead us to advocate a criminal justice system that depends upon perjury as necessary behavior? What possible sense does it make, then, for Christians to justify a system which extols and manipulates individual acquisitiveness and greed, and to call such a system morally right because it is built upon the foundation of human selfishness?

As a matter of fact, Evangelicalism has been part and parcel of this economic system, dominated by it in deed as well as thought. Note how much of Evangelicalism's framework of thinking is determined by the values and modes of our economic order, in, for example, the idolization of church growth, the selling of Jesus in various kinds of evangelism, the reduction of the gospel to sales slogans that can be marketed. Central to the church's recovery of a genuine witness to the kingdom of God in this society is the liberation of the church's own thought and life from the captivity of this society's ways of doing business.

The last issue is nationalism. This issue is of particular importance for the shape of the church, and it is one in which Anabaptism and the believers' church tradition have made a real contribution.

One of the clearest New Testament teachings concerns our identity and unity in Christ which transcends all previous lines of division between races, classes, sexes, and nations. The gospel call is for an allegiance to a new kingdom which entails relinquishing a similar allegiance to earthly political kingdoms. Instead of our loyalties first going to the nation, they go first to God's kingdom, and that kingdom involves us with all humanity, not just with a favorite nation. The interests of all humanity are to receive the priority of the Christian. This is how we reflect God's love for the world. So our view of the world is not to be equated with any particular nation's interests, aims, and perspectives—especially our own. Our hopes no longer rest upon the success of the nation.

This fundamentally new mind set is to be the possession and characteristic of the church which lives in a wholly new order. God's action in history is viewed from a radically different perspective. In fact, it is assumed that the interests of the world's most wealthy nation—and in recent history, most violent nation—are likely to be incompatible with God's purposes for all of humanity. So one's loyalty to the kingdom of God may end up, in all honesty, producing what many consider a form of un-Americanism. Christ becomes politically subversive. If Christ's mandate includes a call to build *His* kingdom, our concrete efforts of ministry, witness, evangelism, and church renewal will inevitably have the effect of undermining any established political, economic, and social order which is alien to that mandate. Such subversion is not a political end in itself. Rather it is the means by which God's justice and love can be extended to all humanity.

In conclusion, all of this leads me to the imperative of building the church. That is the place to begin. It is not the only thing to do, but it is the first thing to do. There is an irony in this for me. For the past few years most of my energies have been spent in the political arena, and that experience has made me all the more radical politically in terms of the questions we face. Now I find myself talking and working at the task of building and renewing the church. But this is not because I have become in any way less political. Indeed, my life has become more involved than ever in political struggles, defined in the broadest and truest sense. I now see, however, that the political task has its starting point in the calling of a people to be faithful to a vision, faithful to the shape and character of God's own entry into the world in Christ. The building of faith communities which detach people from the dominating values and loyalties of worldly society by attaching them to this vision of the kingdom of God is a radical political action. It is at the same time a deeply and thoroughly spiritual creation— the work of the Spirit of God.

In all of this to discover what it means to be radical or authentic disciples we need to recover an authentic heritage to nurture and sustain us. I believe that heritage is simply the biblical tradition—the tradition of Abraham who left the immediate securities that were around him and headed out on a journey of faith to a new land, the tradition of Moses who understood that it was God's purpose to lead people out of economic and social bondage and into liberation, the tradition of the prophets who pleaded with those who claimed to know God to structure their corporate life according to the demands of God's justice and compassion for the distressed and poor. It is the tradition of the disciples who left all for the sake of their Lord and His kingdom and struggled to learn how to love one another as He had loved them. It is the tradition of Paul who spent his life building the church as a community which would manifest the freedom of Christ from the domination of the world. It is the tradition of John, the author of *Revelation,* who was not afraid to see the reality of corporate demonic evil at those places closest to home and still have the capacity to hope and live in the light of God's reign over all. It is the tradition of the early church which knew a radically new form of corporate life in Christ. It did not shrink from suffer-

ing and demonstrated something of the revolutionary
social and political impact of being Christ's life in the
world.

Insofar as the Evangelical churches in America have
repressed this tradition, they have cut themselves off
from their own source of life. But within Evangelicalism,
as elsewhere, are those who have rediscovered, embraced, and are attempting to live out this vision. From
them there is solid ground for hope of fully rebuilding
the church's life and witness.

CHAPTER 5

The Evangelical Factor in American Politics

John A. Lapp

The term "Evangelical" conjures up a variety of images. Two primary ones are the concern for careful formulation of Christian doctrine and the aggressive promotion of the Christian message. Evangelical in this regard is a religious phenomena. Rarely do we think of Evangelical as a political phenomena. Those with a sense of history will recall the potent impact of the "evangelical revival" in England two centuries ago which helped abolish slavery, reformed the penal system, generated the factory acts, and helped stimulate public education. In the American past the evangelical movement has been scarcely less eventful.

The story of American Evangelicalism is the story of America itself in the years 1800 to 1900, for it was Evangelical religion which made Americans the most religious people in the world, molded them into a unified, pietistic-

John A. Lapp is professor of history and dean of Goshen College. The author of *A Dream for America* (Herald Press, 1976), he formerly served as executive secretary of the Mennonite Central Committee Peace Section.

perfectionist nation, and spurred them on to those heights
of social reform, missionary endeavors and imperialistic ex-
pansionism which constitute the moving forces of our history in that century.[1]

This paper is an exploration of the evangelical factor in
the politics of the 1970s. It is not possible to be definitive.
We are too close to the times themselves to understand
all the forces at work. I will try to demonstrate various dimensions of the evangelical factor as a way of gaining
insight rather than total explanation. While I appreciate
the attempt to relate religious and moral criteria to
political life, it will be apparent that I have a fundamental disagreement with the prevailing evangelical approach.

As readers of this volume know, defining the term and
movement known as Evangelical is not easy, especially so
in exploring the politics rather than dogma of this movement. I am using the term for those conservative
Protestants whose identity centers in the organization
known as the National Association of Evangelicals, the
periodical *Christianity Today,* and in the ministry of
Billy Graham. Richard Pierard, an evangelical historian,
suggests that "the confessing Evangelical differs from
the Fundamentalist particularly in that he is seriously
trying to place conservative Christianity in the mainstream of contemporary life and make the Orthodox position a live option for modern man.[2] While there is rich
variety in terms of denominational affiliation, geographic
location, age, and status, there is also enough commonality that one can consider an "evangelical factor."
There are various estimates as to numbers involved.
Time and *Newsweek* magazines use the figure of 40 to 50
million. I will be dealing with mainstream and politically

conservative evangelicals, rather than with the imaginative politics of the "radical evangelicals," an important biblical corrective.

It should be observed that the close link of religion to politics in American society is not new. Already in the 1830s Alexis de Tocqueville noted that "religion in America takes no direct part in the government of society, but it must be regarded as the first of their political institutions."[3] This, of course, also reflected the astute French thinker's understanding that "there is in each religion a political doctrine which, by affinity, is joined to it."[4]

In an age of presumed secularity or at least a time and place where religion and politics are expected to exist apart from each other, de Tocqueville's observations may seem strange. Yet an increasing number of social and political analysts are recognizing that religion and politics do continue to intersect. Indeed, the fact that John Kennedy in 1960 and Jimmy Carter in 1976 had to say, "I never tried to use my position as a public official to promote my beliefs and I never would," indicates that the intimate relationship continues into the late twentieth century.[5]

Electoral Politics

In December 1977 the columnists Evans and Novak titled one of their commentaries, "Carter Seeks Graham's Political Guidance."[6] In the first paragraph they observed "an ecumenical link with political overtones between the powerful evangelical Christian movement and the American Jewish community has caused President Carter to seek guidance from Billy Graham." This suggestion of a "link with political overtones" referred to evangelical support of a strongly pro-Israeli foreign policy.

This role of counseling an American President is not new for Billy Graham, who has visited with all presidents from Harry Truman to Jimmy Carter. Graham, best known for his friendship and defense of Richard Nixon, actually visited the Johnson White House more frequently. Lowell D. Streiker and Gerald S. Strober in a 1972 volume, *Religion and the New Majority*, pointed to Graham as standing "in the closest proximity to the Presidency, to the majority of the nation's Protestants and to the great center of America's social and political life" (p. 39). These authors saw Graham as more than revivalist or White House "chaplain" for he is "today the leader of the political decisive majority" (p. 109).

The idea of Middle America as a New Majority has gone into eclipse since the demise of Richard Nixon. Yet one of the best ways to understand the Carter-Ford campaign of 1976 is to see this battle between the "born again" as a struggle for the Middle American evangelical vote. Presidential campaigns are as much struggles between symbols and images as between political points of view. "Born again" was the symbolical term first suggested by Carter campaign literature but soon picked up by Ford as well. Each candidate visited the largest evangelical convention, the Southern Baptist convention, which met in Norfolk. The religious and secular press kept referring to the religious qualities of the candidates as well as the religious character of the campaign. The headlines tell the story: "Will Evangelicals Swing the Election" (*Christianity Today*, June 18); "Carter Evangelism (sic) Putting Religion into Politics for First Time Since 1960," (*New York Times*, June 5); "God and the

GOP at Kansas City" (*Christianity Today*, September 10); "Crusade for the White House: Skirmishes in a Holy War" (*Christianity Today*, November 19).

The point is not that the headlines or the analysis are completely accurate. Indeed there were misperceptions especially as secular journalists tried to understand the depth and strength of religious commitment. There were class and regional differences between the appeals of a Baptist (Carter) and Episcopal (Ford), and Presbyterian (Reagan). But Michael Novak (not to be confused with the columnist Robert Novak) was not far from the mark when he wrote in the *Washington Post* (April 4, 1976) that "the most understated demographic reality in the U.S. is the huge number of evangelical Protestants, Jimmy Carter's natural constituency."

Analyzing voting returns is never simple or apparent. Because of bloc voting it is possible to consider blacks, Jews, or Catholics as the critical factor. Albert Menendez, who analyzed the religious factor in this election, noted 10 heavily evangelical counties in Missouri where Kennedy won by 38 percent, and Carter by 55 percent. Sensing the same voter shifts in Ohio, Tennessee, Kentucky, and Pennsylvania, Menendez says, "Carter was unbeatable." Menendez cites the CBS News survey which gave Carter "46 percent of the Protestant vote, a gain of 7 percent over the 1952-1972 average Democratic Presidental vote among Protestants."[7] Ford, like most of his Republican predecessors, won the majority of both Protestant and evangelical votes but it was a much closer contest than during the past 30 years.

What this suggests is that religion does play an important role in American politics. The irony is that contrary to the expectations of 1972, the decisive bloc was not captive to one party but open to the appeal of an evangelical candidate in either party.

Evangelical influence has been felt in a number of congressional elections and local issues. Evangelicals like Anita Bryant and Ron Adrian have rallied voters against local ordinances guaranteeing civil rights to avowed homosexuals. Strongly evangelical persons have been conspicuous spokesmen in Congress, for example, John Conlan of Arizona, John B. Anderson of Illinois, Albert H. Quie of Minnesota, Mark Hatfield of Oregon, Harold Hughes, formerly of Iowa.

The recent primary struggle in the Illinois 16th Congressional district illustrates the difficulty in talking about one evangelical factor. Representative John B. Anderson, a member of the Evangelical Covenant Church, has been in Congress for 18 years. He is the third ranking Republican in the House of Representatives, a moderate who took leadership in promoting civil rights legislation and more recently supported the Panama Canal treaty. He has spoken frequently in evangelical contexts and has written a widely read paperback entitled *Vision and Betrayal in America* (1975) where among other things, he celebrates the new influence of evangelicals.

Yet in the March Republican primary Anderson was challenged by Don Lyon, pastor of an Open Bible Church who assailed the liberal voting record of Anderson. Both candidates spent over $150,000 to get on the November ballot with Anderson finally winning with the help of Democratic voters who crossed over to express their distaste of Lyon.

Lyon was strongly supported by Richard Viguerie, a fund raiser for George Wallace and other right-wing candidates. Viguerie, a Roman Catholic, sees "the next real major area of growth for the conservative ideology and (political) philosophy among evangelical people." This movement will succeed only if moderates are replaced by true blue individuals "to give conservatives somebody to vote for in November."[8]

Influence Peddlers

Evangelical political power can be felt at a number of other places other than on election day. In a day of mass media the making and molding of public opinion is a more significant factor in determining political action than exercising the franchise itself. Those institutions and individuals who can get their point of view carried by the airwaves or on the printed page exert a power that has been likened to the "fourth branch" of government.

Time and *Newsweek* magazines have both featured "Evangelical" Christianity during the past two years. The "evangelical empire," to use the language of *Time* (December 26, 1977) is nowhere more apparent than the enormous energy now expended on television and radio programming. The National Religious Broadcasters Association reported that at the end of 1977 there were 1, 064 religious radio stations and 25 similar television stations. They estimate a listening audience of 114 million on the radio and a viewing audience of 14 million. Both media are growing. There is a similar boom in religious publishing, especially those books stocked in the Christian Booksellers Association stores.

There have been repeated attempts to use religiously based groups to influence public policy. Ever since the turn of the century "social gospel" movement, the major denominations have discussed political issues in their periodicals and have frequently addressed specific policy questions. The campaign for prohibition was a high point of Protestant political power. The National Council of Churches and the National Association of Evangelicals have had Washington offices to monitor national and international developments. During the 1960s churches were active participants in the struggle for racial justice and against the war in Vietnam. At the same time large numbers of conservative evangelicals either said these issues were not the business of the church or actively opposed racial justice and the peace movement.

The spokesman for conservative Christians apart from the NAE Washington office, tended to be right-wing organizations and personalities who mixed their conservative theological views with conservative political positions. Some of the better known are Billy James Hargis and the Christian Crusade, Carl McIntyre and the 20th Century Reformation Hour, Fred Schwartz and the Christian Anti-Communist Crusade, Gerald L. K. Smith and the Christian Nationalist Crusade, Howard Kerchner and Christian Freedom Foundation. During the 1960s over 25 major Christian organizations on the political right had annual budgets of over $14 million. Most of these groups promoted an aggressive Americanism and saw a conspiracy in Washington and New York that was leading the country toward communism. They had links to essentially secular right-wing organizations like the John Birch Society.

By the early 1970s most of the above mentioned groups lost their own power as conservatives felt they had a patron in Richard Nixon and hence moved into electoral politics rather than promoting causes. The growing respectability of Evangelicals and Evangelicalism led to more activity within the organized denominations and political parties, less through independent congregations and third parties.

With the demise of Nixon there has been a resurgence by the political right. For the most part the most vigorous advocates work within essentially political bodies such as the Committee for the Survival of a Free Congress, Citizens for the Republic, and the National Conservative Political Action Committee.

Sojourners editors Jim Wallis and Wes Michaelson in a major article, "The Plan to Save America: A Disclosure of an Alarming Political Initiative by the Evangelical Far Right" (April 1976) documented the connections between the political and religious right wing. Their report centered on a group of wealthy and influential Evangelical leaders. In February 1976 this group opened the Christian Embassy in Washington for the explicit purpose of evangelizing government officials. Bill Bright, head of Campus Crusade, in the dedicatory address declared that America had forsaken God and "unless there is a great turning to God, God will use a great atheistic power like Russia to chasten us." If there can be a revival of Christian people "then we'll see the revival of the patriotic spirit that we need so badly."[9]

The same group of Bright; John B. Conlan, former U.S. Representative from Arizona; Richard De Vos, president of Amway; and a journalist, Rus Walton, founded Third Century Publishers in 1974 to "promote conservative political views based on scriptural principles." Their major publications include *One Nation Under God*, written by Walton, and *In the Spirit of '76*, a handbook for winning elections. The monthly *Third Century Report* promotes conservative positions and candidates and analyzes voting records of Congress-men. This group strongly supported Ronald Reagan for the Republican nomination for the presidency in 1976 and works closely with the already mentioned Richard Viguerie in his campaign for a conservative Congress.

The Christian Freedom Foundation, which long pub-lished *Christian Economics,* and later *Applied Christian-ity,* was taken over by John Conlan in 1974. The founda-tion, which provides an organizational cover for a variety of activities, is also the link of this new movement to the right wing of the 1950s and 1960s. How much money is being raised and expended on these causes is unclear. We know the Christian Embassy cost over $1 million to get established. Viguerie takes in millions of dollars for conservative Congressional candidates.

As already noted in the campaign to oust John Ander-son, the evangelical right is not always successful and indeed sometimes splits Evangelicals into two political groupings. There is some indication that Billy Graham and Bill Bright differ on both tactics and positions. Indeed John Conlan openly attacks evangelical Harold Hughes and Mark Hatfield as extreme left-wingers.

Evangelical power is not only expressed in Wash-ington, but in state and local organizations. One area de-serving further study is the close links of American evan-gelicals with conservative politicans abroad. Bill Bright, for example, has been a vigorous defender of the present regime in South Korea. Billy Graham in a recent tour to East Asia was given a state dinner by President Ferdi-nand Marcos of the Philippines. Other names could be cited for their close advocacy ties of existing regimes in Taiwan, Zaire, Rhodesia, and Vietnam before 1975. These relationships have not only helped determine public opinion in the U.S. but on occasion have influenced the making of foreign policy. Evangelical support of the state of Israel has been a visible force in that nation's continuing struggle.

Ideological Matrix

Bill Bright, whom we already identified, published *Your Five Duties as a Christian Citizen* in 1976. This booklet (available through Christians Concerned for More Responsible Citizenship, P.O. Box 3009, San Bernardino, California) summarizes in a concise way the key political concepts of Evangelicals.

The first duty is to pray. Pray "that God will send a great spiritual awakening to America." Pray "to live a godly life." Pray "daily that God will change or remove from positions of public leadership officials who are godless, carnal and disobedient to Him, so that righteous leadership will be restored and America will turn from her wicked ways." Pray for the election of godly people to public office.

The second duty is to register to vote "in order to practice your citizenship with accountability to God." Voting which helps insure godly officials "is a matter of stewardship under God." The third duty is to become informed concerning government, current problems, and issues, and "how to serve God effectively in the arena of politics." You must know how to act for His glory within the framework of existing political processes." Start a study group on Christian citizenship. "Delay can be fatal to America."

The fourth duty is to help elect godly people, "the most effective way to restore righteous rule and rejoicing in America." This can best be done by becoming "a precinct leader." "There are only approximately 175,000 precincts in the U.S.: thus, a relatively few godly people can help to change the direction of this nation."

Finally, "vote consistently in every election, after informing yourself concerning the various candidates and issues, and evaluating them on the basis of the Word of God."

Throughout the booklet Bright emphasizes the precarious condition of the nation and the need for urgent action now. For the conclusion he observed the bravery of those who signed the Declaration of Independence suggesting how they could have been convicted as traitors and that this same kind of zeal is now necessary: "We dare not fail them, ourselves, and far more important, our Lord, to whom this nation was dedicated. Our nation is now faced with its greatest crisis in history. If ever you plan to do anything for Christ and America, please do it now."

From this booklet and reading in other materials put out by Evangelicals, it is possible to discern the key political ideas of most Evangelicals. First there are the assumptions of orthodox theology focusing on the transcendent God, revelation in Christ, individual salvation, and the presence of evil. Second, there is the high view of government in which using the existing processes for citizenship is "accountability to God." This is an arena where God acts through His people. As Billy James Hargis put it: "Christ is the heart of the conservative cause. We conservatives are fighting for God and country."[10]

The third and central idea claims that America is a Christian nation. The entire tone of the Bright leaflet suggests this. Billy Graham in his Honor America Day address, July 4, 1970, stated this conviction as his last reason for honoring America:

> We honor America because there is woven into the warp and woof of our nation faith in God. The ethical and moral principles of the Judeo-Christian faith and the God of that tradition are found throughout the Declaration of Independence. Most presidents of the U.S. have declared their faith in God and have encouraged us to read the Bible. I am encouraged to believe that Americans at this hour are striving to retain their spiritual identity despite the inroads of materialism and the rising tide of permissiveness.[11]

Fourth, while evangelical politics has its certainties, it also feels threatened by some force or forces internal and external. Hence the repeated references to "crisis" and the feeling that a conspiracy is undermining the pillars of stability. Since World War II most of the fear has centered on communism but at other times it has been big government bankers, Jews, intellectuals, and the United Nations. John H. Redekop in his excellent study of Billy James Hargis quotes Hargis as saying, "I fight Communism . . . because it is part of my ordination vows, of my creed."[12]

Although other ideas help organize this political creed these remain the core Evangelical political concepts. Each sector, however, may organize its ideas differently and emphasize one feature over another.

Two other factors need mentioning. The more extreme the statement the more likely there will be heavy apocalyptic overtones. The expectation of an imminent cataclysm provides emotional fervor and makes possible clear division between the good and bad, the ins and outs. Second, it is worth noting that evangelical

skepticism regarding social change fits well with the rising social status. Richard Pierard sees rightests and conservatives speaking "for the privileged classes in American society; they are firmly committed to American nationalism, limited government and the preservation of
property rights and have a built-in resistance to
change."[13]

Richard Quebedeaux summarizes establishment evangelical politics this way:

> By and large, 20th Century white, evangelicals have either
> been outwardly apolitical or have taken the conservative
> position on almost every social, economic, and political
> issue. For a long time there has been a visible alliance
> between the evangelical right and center and the Re-
> publican Party, culminating perhaps in the Billy Graham-
> Richard Nixon friendship and the evangelist's public en-
> dorsement of Nixon's presidential candidacy in 1972.[14]

It is not part of our story but mention must be made
that the evangelical tradition has not always been considered politically conservative. David Moberg calls the
shift to this position "The Great Reversal" because in
pre-Civil War days evangelical revivalism actively joined
and often led campaigns to abolish slavery, establish
public education, and struggle for a higher public morality. Indeed it was not until the 1920s when evangelicals as a bloc became identified as conservative defenders of the status quo.

An Unequal Yoke?

How then are we to understand and evaluate the
politics of modern Evangelicalism? Is this an unusual
phenomena in the history of Christianity or on the

American scene? Are the Evangelicals' understandings biblical? Is their alignment indeed what Richard Pierard calls an "unequal yoke" or Richard Quebedeaux calls "worldly"?

First of all it is important to observe that Evangelicals are neither the first nor likely the last Christian party to align themselves with a rather clearly defined political position. Indeed since the days of Constantine in the fourth century of the Christian era the church in most places in most times has been part of a political social establishment. The churches in colonial America except in Pennsylvania were part of an established order. Even after constitutional disestablishment the notion of a Christian society persisted. Sidney Mead, the distinguished historian of Christianity in America noted:

> that at the time Protestantism in America achieved its greatest dominance of the culture (1850-1900) it had also achieved an almost complete ideological and emotional identification with the burgeoning bourgeois society and its free enterprise system, so that in 1876 Protestantism presented a massive, almost unbroken front in its defense of the status quo. [15]

Evangelicals who link their faith to conservative politics are continuing a well-developed tradition.

Second, it is worth noting that the conservative Protestants' view of society is not essentially different from the American way of life mentality of liberal groups. George Williams and Rodney Peterson put it starkly: "Modernist/liberals and fundamentalists/evangelicals have not essentially disagreed about the American state as having a special place in their theology of history or theodicy if not in their systematic theology." [16]

Whatever critique we make of evangelicals in politics it is one that can be made of Protestants in general. What is different is that Evangelicals who felt alienated from the majority both politically and religiously since the denominational divisions of the 1920s now are again in the mainstream of American life. Their churches are growing and their politicans are winning elections. John Anderson, even though he can be critical of the narrow conservatism of coreligionists, nevertheless suggests the new psychology:

> It was they (the liberals) who denied the supernatural acts of God, conforming the gospel to the canons of modern science. It was they who advocated laws and legislation as the modern substitutionary atonement for the sins of mankind. . . . It was they who were the friends of those in positions of political power. They were the "beautiful people," and we—you will recall—were the "kooks." We were regarded as rural, reactionary, illiterate fundamentalists who just didn't know better.
> Well, things have changed. Now they are the "kooks"— and we are the "beautiful people." Our prayer breakfasts are so popular that only those with engraved invitations are allowed to attend. Our evangelists have the ready ear of those in positions of highest authority. Our churches are growing and theirs are withering. . . . They are tired, worn-out 19th Century liberals trying to repair the pieces of an optimism shattered by world wars, race riots, population explosion, and the spectre of worldwide famine. We always knew that things would get worse before the Lord came again.[17]

How do we explain this new surge of self-confidence and influence? That topic is an essay in itself, but several suggestions are possible. One reason is certainly the exhaustion of the liberal establishment. Another the dislocation people feel in the face of rapid social change and international turmoil. In a time of confusion and testing the Evangelical spirit provides a sense of purpose and confidence. As Jorstad said of the radical right, this "furnishes the assurance that they are the only Christians in America and only their program can save the nation from self-destruction."[18] In the backlash from the reforming zeal of the 1960s, Evangelicals provide a new conservative culture with "meaning, belonging and identity apparently over against other Americans which on the other hand, are taught to fit in with the other Americans to be the real and true citizens".[19]

Finally, I want to suggest four ways where to me the prevailing evangelical political stance is found wanting. First, the repeated desire to restore or return to a nobler more Christian politics reflects a serious misreading of history. The past had its imperfections and injustices. The remote past was really no better than the recent past now being repudiated. Second, the desire to infuse political activity with highly moral and religious language tends to sacralize the political order which is precisely the opposite of the biblical intention. The political order is the arena of the penultimate, not the ultimate. As John Redekop noted of Billy James Hargis, the threat lies "in the failure to distinguish between the finality of ultimate, divine authority and the partial insight of the human purveyor."[20]

Third, Evangelicals in politics tend toward a confrontationist style. Political campaigns and international conflicts are viewed in rigid polarities of right and wrong with the right organized for the vengeance of holy war. Fourth, and most basic, each of the above is possible because the gospel is individualized and privatized because of an inadequate understanding of the church as the first fruits of the new creation. At the same time the pessimism and passivity which characterizes Evangelical eschatology depreciates the possibility of social reform and political change. As Pierard says, this linkage "prevents the Gospel from exercising its fullest effectiveness in modern society."[21]

Yet I want to conclude on a hopeful note. The wonderful characteristic of the Christian movement is its potential for renewal. The sharpest criticisms of Evangelical politics are made by Evangelicals themselves. Some of the freshest, most vigorous formulations for Christian faithfulness in the political arena are being made by thoughtful and courageous Evangelicals. There can well be another "Great Reversal."

CHAPTER 6

The Inerrancy Controversy
Within Evangelicalism

J. C. Wenger

It is a major error to begin quibbling over the proper
name for our doctrine of inspiration without first assert-
ing our faith in a God who in love and grace has chosen
to reveal Himself to us through the prophets in a preparatory manner, and fully and definitively in His incarnate Son, the Lord Jesus Christ. Indeed, God has
given some revelation of Himself through the world
which He has created, including man whom He made in
His own image (Romans 1:20; Genesis 1:26). "The
heavens are telling the glory of God" (Psalm 19:1-6).
This same God revealed Himself in the history of Israel.
He called Abram to leave the highly civilized Ur and to
become His pilgrim disciple, following His leading all
the way to Canaan, where he dwelt in tents, confessing
that his real home was not on earth. For his gaze was
fixed on God and the eternal city in the heavens (Hebrews 11:8-10). Likewise God led Israel out of Egypt and

J. C. Wenger is professor of historical theology at Goshen Biblical
Seminary. Author of *God's Word Written* (Herald Press, 1966) and
numerous other titles, he is a bishop in the Mennonite Church and a
popular speaker.

established them as His covenant people.

Further, the faith of Christian believers is not a logical deduction; it is not based on a consideration of the traditional theistic proofs: cosmological, teleological, ontological, and moral. It is rather God's work through the gracious inner witness of the Holy Spirit who is pleased to use the witness of the creation, and especially the testimony of the holy Scriptures, to awaken conviction for sin, and to nudge the sinner toward a surrender to Christ as Savior and Lord. The acceptance of the Bible as the Word of God is not the end of a chain of logic. It is much more the discovery of Christ through the witness of the Scriptures that God has spoken, first through the prophets of old, and later by His Son.

The Nature of Scripture

It is fully legitimate to speak of the Bible as the Word of God, for the writers of the New Testament do so. The author of *Hebrews* calls upon his readers not to forget the warning of Psalm 95: "Harden not your hearts." We had better take heed to this divine warning, he adds, for "the word of God is living and active, sharper than any two-edged sword" (Hebrews 4:12). But the writer of *Hebrews* did not initiate this concept. For its origin we must go back to our Lord Himself. In the Fourth Gospel when Christ was accused of blasphemy because He called Himself God, in a sort of *argumentum ad hominem*, Christ appealed to the fact that in the Old Testament Scriptures VIPs were called *Elohim* ("gods"). "If He called them *Elohim,* unto whom the *word of God* came (and *Scripture* cannot be broken), do you say of Him whom the Father sanctified and sent into the world, 'You blaspheme,' because I said that I am the Son of God?"

(John 10:35 f.). For our Lord it seemed to be self-evident that the Scriptures were identical with the divine Word which came to Israel of old. It was the assumption of Christ and the apostles that the Scriptures were the very Word of God.

But Christians must not overlook the paradoxical truth that the Scriptures were in their entirety written by men. They were holy men, to be sure, men of faith. But they were human. And the Bible contains a remarkable variety of literary types. It contains God's gracious instruction known as the Torah or law. It has a considerable amount of history, the account of God's special people who bore His name: Abraham and the patriarchs, Israel through all her lights and shadows, and finally the New Israel of God, the Christian church. The Bible contains wisdom literature such as Ecclesiastes, ethical maxims such as the Book of Proverbs, poetry such as the Book of Psalms, allegories such as the trees walking to a conference to choose a king (Judges 9), parables such as those in Matthew 13, drama such as the Book of Job and much of the Apocalypse, theodicy such as Habakkuk, theological essays such as Hebrews, word portraits of the Son of God in His incarnate life—the four Gospels, and a vast number of letters. Twenty out of twenty-seven of the New Testament books are personal letters.

And the several books of the Bible contain an amazing number of figures of speech, some of them just as earthy as those of today. For example, Jesus used a metaphor when He called Herod Antipas a "fox," for stealing his brother Philip's wife (Luke 13:32). We have metonymy when "Moses and the prophets" refers to their writings rather than to them as persons (Luke 16:29). Then there is synecdoche when "the cup" points to what its contents stand for (1 Corinthians 11:25). Hyperbole is illustrated by a large gathering being described as "the whole city" (Mark 1:33); and dying is described by the euphemism, "he fell asleep" (Acts 7:60). But the most common figure in Scripture is the idiom—a form of speech which is clear to its hearers but which needs interpretation or explanation when translated. A "pain in the neck" in English means a trial or annoyance to a person. It is not literal pain, nor does it relate to the neck. Examples of Hebrew idioms would be "uncovering the ear" which meant making known to, and "putting words into someone's mouth" meant telling them what to say.

The Scriptures were written within and accurately represent the specific historical context, and each portion must be understood by the light which historical research throws on its own period. Because each writer wrote in a given context, the more we can know about that historical milieu the better off we will be in rightly understanding the writings of that period. In our era, for example, expressions such as the "stars and stripes," the "hammer and the sickle," the "crescent and the sword," and the more playful "Uncle Sam," are readily recognized. Perhaps the "hornet" of Deuteronomy 7:20 meant Egypt, for in the hieroglyphics of that era the writer wishing to identify Lower Egypt drew a bee. Similarly the *pim* of 1 Samuel 13:21 was a riddle to all translators until modern archaeologists found a number of stones (weights) with "pim" inscribed on them. It should be evident that to arrive at the true meaning of many biblical statements calls for the employment of the grammatico-historical exegesis of the original tongues of Holy Scripture. Failing such a linguistic help, the use of a variety of good versions is most helpful.

But even after we decode the ancient figures of speech, and after we begin to master some of the major historical allusions of a given writer, there are still a vast number of statements which reflect human emotions, responses, reasoning, prayers, hopes, fears, and aspirations, for the Bible is from beginning to end both human and divine—not partly human and partly divine, but *wholly human* and *wholly divine*. The Spirit of God was active in its total writing, just as were its human authors. If the "humanity" of the Bible is denied or overlooked, we distort a true doctrine of Scripture by making it "docetic"[1]—and that is just as much an error as to deny that our Lord was both fully divine and fully human.

The role of the human writer varied as widely in the writing of holy Scripture as do the various types of literature which comprise the "Oracles of God." The writer may be recording holy history as recited in the well-known summaries in Israel (Deuteronomy 26:5-9), or he may be dictating a summary of the divine oracles received from the Lord (Jeremiah 36:32), or he may be recording the results of his research (Luke 1:1-4), or he may be giving a reasoned plea for the unity of the people of God (1 Corinthians 3). Origen (c. 185-c. 254) was right when he declared of the biblical writings, "All are divine, and human are they all." There was a tendency in the ancient church to forget this obvious truth—and the tendency is still with us!

The Scriptures in the Ancient Church

The early church evidently assumed that everyone knew that the Bible was written by men; it was the divine activity in the writing of Scripture, they believed, which required emphasis. Clement, bishop of Rome during the closing decade of the first century AD, therefore described the Scriptures as "the true utterances of the Holy Spirit." The Epistle of Barnabas of the second century introduced scriptural citations with "the Spirit of the Lord proclaims." Polycarp (c. 69-155) referred to the Scriptures as "The oracles of the Lord." Justin Martyr of the second century declared, "We believe God's voice, spoken by the apostles ... and prophets." Athenagoras of the second century stated flatly that the Holy Spirit used the biblical writers "as a flute player might blow a flute."[2] Irenaeus of the latter second century held that although the Bible was written by human beings, it was nevertheless ultimately divine, and the divine charisma (anointing or gift) insured its reliability. Indeed, said he, the various voices of the biblical writers constitute a symphony of truth! Augustine (354-430) held that the very words of Scripture (in the original tongues) are divinely trustworthy. He acknowledged that there was no perfect translation, and that the manuscripts of the contemporary (Old) Latin version were especially poor. He was emphatic that spiritual truth depends on the divine authority of the Scriptures: "Faith will totter if the authority of Scripture begins to shake." He also wrote, "If I do find anything in these books which seems contrary to truth, I decide that either the text is corrupt, or the translator did not follow what was really said, or that I failed to understand it."[3]

By way of summary we may quote J. T. Forestall from the *New Catholic Encyclopedia:* "It was the unanimous teaching of the Fathers that the Sacred Scriptures were free from error, and from all contradiction." He adds, "The canonical Scriptures were always considered to be in a class apart."[4]

The Scripture in the Reformation

In the long period between Augustine and Luther the scholarship of the church decayed. The medieval scholars delighted in collecting comments from many ancient writers on a given doctrine or passage of Scripture. Theology tended to be a strange fusion of Aristotelian science with biblical revelation. Furthermore, great emphasis was laid on the church as the official interpreter of Scripture—a view to which Augustine assented, although Augustine knew that churchmen, and even councils, could err.

It may be noted in passing that the understanding of the doctrines of the church and of the Christian life in such medieval "prophets" as Waldo (c. 1200), Wycliffe (c. 1325-1384), Hus (martyred 1415), and Chelčicky (c. 1390-1457) were remarkably similar in some respects to those of the sixteenth-century Anabaptists, particularly on the so-called "hard sayings" of our Lord—on wealth-seeking, the oath, claiming titles of veneration, discipleship as cross-bearing, and discipleship to the nonresistant Prince of Peace.

The Reformers of the sixteenth century—Luther, Zwingli, and Calvin—had to fight a battle for the sole authority of Scripture. Catholicism had a two-source theory of authority: (1) the Bible and (2) ecclesiastical tradition. (This dual source was made dogma at the Council of Trent, 1545-63.) The Reformers therefore had much to say about the Bible as sole authority in faith and life (*sola scriptura*). This was a battle which had to be fought, but one of their tragic mistakes, in the eyes of the Anabaptists, was to employ the Old Testament as an attenuating force on the ethical teachings of Christ. The Old Testament was appealed to to justify the persecution of dissenters (e.g. Deuteronomy 13), to defend the baptism of infants by a comparison with Old Testament circumcision, to continue the swearing of oaths, and to justify Christians in the waging of "just" wars. Most Evangelicals today still understand the Bible this way.

Modernism and Its Gospel

Historically, the effort to determine the original text of Scripture was known as lower criticism, while the studies of authorship, date, and unity were called higher criticism. During the nineteenth century a goodly number of German scholars, who were influenced by rationalism, began to doubt the possibility of miracles, and on that ground they rejected the virgin birth of our Lord, as well as His bodily resurrection. By the same token belief in His personal return to raise the dead and judge the world was also given up.

Edwin Arthur Burtt, himself a humanist by conviction, regarded the four main roots of Modernism to be the theory of organic evolution, the higher criticism of the Bible, the comparative study of religion, and modern humanistic psychology.[5] Let us look briefly at each of these.

In 1859 Charles Darwin (1809-1882) published his famous work, *On the Origin of Species by Means of Natural Selection*, and followed in 1871 with his monograph, *The Descent of Man*. Originally educated at Edinburgh and Cambridge for the Christian ministry, Darwin had turned to science, and he became an outstanding naturalist. Darwin saw life forms emerging in history from more primitive and simple forms, all of which were struggling for survival. Those best adapted for survival were able to make it, while the forms unable to adapt became extinct. Coupled with this struggle to survive was the

constant appearance of new variations which contributed
to the emergence of new forms. Even before Darwin, the
concept of a "natural law" which would allow no divine
intrusion into the natural order was becoming established. Now the bold new theory of Darwin seemed to
account for man's unique gifts apart from any doctrine of
special creation. Those who came to be regarded as
Modernists attempted to cling to some form of theism
while making room for Darwinism at the same time.

The name of Julius Wellhausen (1844-1918) is closely
associated with the rise of higher criticism. Wellhausen
saw the development of the Old Testament literature
through the eyes of a believer in the evolution of religion.
He ventured the theory that there was almost no Hebrew
literature prior to 1000 BC, except some war and march
songs, some proverbs, riddles, and fables, and some prophetic blessings and oracles. He cut the Old Testament
into an infinite number of sources and fragments, and
scattered them down through history from the ninth to
the second century BC.[6] According to his theory divine
revelation gives way to the evolution of religion along
largely naturalistic lines. Israel began with a tribal deity
like other Canaanite groups and slowly climbed up to
ethical monotheism.

The third root of Modernism was the comparative
study of religion. One of the great names in this field is
Sir James George Frazer (1854-1941), author of a twelve-
volume work on "cults, rites, and myths," and how they
contributed to the rise of various religions. Frazer
condensed his findings into a famous work, *The Golden
Bough*. The "golden bough" on the tree of religion is
Christianity which is viewed as a human, cultural development, based on fear and superstition.

Religion is interpreted as a means of self-integration. A person needs religion, any religion, for the integration of his personality. Salvation is regarded as the deliverance by this inner integration from tensions, guilt, and a lack of peace. It is emancipation from all that makes for personal misery. Christianity, according to this view, is only relatively better than other religions because of the exceptional gifts of a Galilean teacher named Jesus of Nazareth. That is why it is called the "*golden* bough."

The final root of Modernism is modern psychology which sees people as continuous with the animals. A person is not a special creation bearing the spiritual image of God. He is rather a gifted animal with an opposable thumb, keen powers of observation, and a clever capacity to adapt means to ends. The basic assumption is man's total continuity with the animal creation. What theologians call the soul is nonexistent, and the concepts of free will and responsibility to God must be dropped. Personal immortality after death, not to mention the bodily resurrection, are likewise incredible. All these concepts are "unscientific."

What then is left? A great deal, declares the Modernist. The traditional religions have always been a means to bring the individual to inner integration. People need to learn to live by love. They need to exercise kindness and graciousness in relation to each other. They need to cultivate helpfulness to others. They need to help to relate to such tragedies as accidents and untimely deaths in terms of their "naturalness," and the opportunity they give to other people to show loving care.

As with any other position in theology, there are various shades of Modernism from those who have taken

but a few hesitating steps away from historic Christianity
to those who are almost as far down the road as hu-
manists. Indeed, the logical outcome of this line of
thought is religious humanism. But the essence of the
Modernist position is the full acceptance and incorpora-
tion of modern science into one's life and world-view
while holding to faith in God and His goodness.[7]

The Response of Fundamentalism

As the Modernists began to question the traditional
understanding of full biblical authority on such central
issues as the creation of man in the divine image, the
virgin birth, and substitutionary atonement of our Lord,
along with His bodily resurrection and personal return at
the end of the world, various churchmen arose to defend
the historic faith of the church. Shortly before World
War I two wealthy laymen, who were deeply concerned
for the faith, arranged for the publication of twelve paperback volumes of biblical and theological essays called
The Fundamentals. Initially these were sent out free to
many thousands of Christian workers all around the
world. Eventually nearly 3,000,000 copies of these little
volumes were published.[8]

Editors and writers of these volumes included staunch
and able conservative scholars such as James Orr, B. B.
Warfield, G. Campbell Morgan, and M. G. Kyle. Along
with these another emerging group of men came forward
to represent the new fundamentalist movement: A. C.
Dixon, R. A. Torrey, A. T. Pierson, and C. I. Scofield.
Over the years, the critics of the movement felt, Fundamentalism became more and more anti-intellectual,
increasingly inclined to test everyone by their shibboleths such as the verbal and plenary inspiration of the

Scriptures, the premillennial return of Christ, the substitutionary atonement of Christ, and by their attitude toward the "Social Gospel." One of the staunchest defenders of historic Christianity, J. Gresham Machen (1881-1937), was dropped as a member of the Philadelphia Fundamentalist Association because he did not believe in an earthly millennium—one of the agreed-upon fundamentals. As the movement became more and more ingrown, a radical wing developed which insisted on six twenty-four hour days for the creation of the universe, and on the age of the world as six thousand years.

All the while the stricter Protestant bodies, such as Lutheran and Presbyterian, kept on teaching their full-orbed theology which agreed on a number of points with the emphases of the Fundamentalists, but which also differed sharply with other of its emphases. The *Lutheran Cyclopedia*, for example, remarks that "Fundamentalism . . . has, in many of its sectors, embraced chiliasm and other errors."

John Horsch (1867-1941), a private scholar of Scottdale, Pennsylvania, attempted to help his Mennonite denomination see that the Fundamentalists were right in their struggles with the Modernists. Daniel Kauffman (1865-1944), the leading Mennonite churchman of his day, remarked cautiously that Mennonites were fundamentalists "with a small f." Kauffman did not like the eschatology of the Fundamentalists which was strongly influenced by the dispensationalism of C. I. Scofield (1843-1921). He especially rejected Scofield's "postponement theory" which relegated the Sermon on the Mount to "kingdom truth" which was postponed until Christ's earthly millennial reign. Perhaps the most fundamentalistic Mennonite (General Conference) institution founded was Grace Bible Institute of Omaha, Nebraska.

With hindsight we can venture to assert that a number of the men once associated with Fundamentalism would have been more accurately called conservative or orthodox. I have in mind men such as Abraham Kuyper (1837-1920) and Herman Bavinck (1854-1921) of the Netherlands, James Orr (1844-1913) of Scotland, and B. B. Warfield (1851-1921) and J. Gresham Machen (1881-1937) of Princeton. I heard Machen declare that he did not call himself a Fundamentalist, but that on the major theological differences of that movement with modernism, he stood with the conservative [in spite of their rigidities].

As a matter of truth it must be admitted that in the defeat of the older Modernism which tried to reduce Christianity down to God's universal fatherhood and man's universal brotherhood, it was not so much Fundamentalism as scholars like Karl Barth (1886-1968) and Emil Brunner (1889-1966) of Switzerland, Karl Heim (1874-1958) of Germany, and Reinhold Niebuhr (1892-1971) of the U.S.A., who succeeded in getting theologians to take a more serious view of human sinfulness and of Christ's redemption.

Meanwhile a new development has been taking place in America, and to some extent in Great Britain. A number of theological conservatives have begun to call themselves Evangelicals. Typical of this new trend are Edward John Carnell, the late president of Fuller Seminary; Gordon Clark of Butler University; Carl F. H. Henry, who inaugurated *Christianity Today;* Harold John Ockenga, president of Gordon-Conwell Seminary; and Bernard Ramm, a Baptist seminary professor. These

men seek to be just as sound in the faith as the Fundamentalists were, but with a more sensitive conscience on
the social ills which call for Christian action, and with a
greater eagerness to dialogue with those who do not fully
share their convictions on the full trustworthiness of
Scripture, and other evangelical doctrines.

The Nature of Biblical Truth

Today's Evangelicals have had to build into their
thought systems the assured results of scientific research.
Few Evangelical scholars, for example, would doubt the
immense antiquity of the universe, including our galaxy
and our solar system. Likewise, it is evident that man has
been on the earth much longer than earlier Bible scholars
thought. (It should be noted that the orthodox theologian, Charles Hodge of Princeton, declared a hundred
years ago that the antiquity of man had no adverse effect
on Christian theology.) Until the advent of modern
astronomy, no scholar had an inkling of the vastness of
even our galaxy, not to mention the innumerable other
galaxies located at unthinkable distances from ours.
Scientists of today also recognize the infinitely complex
nature of matter, not to mention the vastly more significant complexity of human personhood, which includes
the physical, intellectual, emotional, social, and spiritual
facets of the human personality. Modern learning makes
necessary a far greater Creator than was earlier dreamed
of.

This advance of human learning, coupled with more
careful Bible scholarship, has led to a far more complex
doctrine of Scripture than was earlier recognized.
Indeed, one of the complaints of thorough scholarship is
that Fundamentalism was much too prone to rely on

shibboleths and on extremely brief doctrinal statements rather than to see the need of patient and exhaustive scholarship. Machen's learned biblical monograph on the *Virgin Birth of Christ* in contrast to much Fundamentalist literature recognizes this complexity and the resultant need for scholarship. And Charles Hodge felt he needed three massive volumes to articulate the theology of Christian faith before his death. In contrast Moody Bible Institute felt able to draft a five-article Doctrinal Statement in 1928 consisting of only forty very short lines!

It is increasingly recognized by competent Evangelical scholars that to proclaim one's belief in verbal and plenary inspiration is not an adequate statement of the deep mystery of the confluence of the human and the divine in the production of the Holy Scriptures. Both adjectives, verbal and plenary, can be interpreted in a legitimate sense. But they do not safeguard the doctrine of inspiration from being understood in a mechanical sense, as if the Spirit of God had dictated the Word line by line. (Although Calvin employed the word *dictate,* it is clear from his many qualifications that he was far from holding to what is now recognized as dictation.) The theologian must be careful to recognize fully both the actual human writer and the mysterious activity of the Holy Spirit which makes it possible to describe the books of both the Old and New Testaments as the very Word of God. Otherwise he will wind up with a docetic doctrine of Scripture.

It is true that the ancient doctrine of Scripture tended to minimize the role of the human writers. This is especially evident in those churchmen, for example, who compared the role of the human writers to the plectrum of a musician! Although the Reformers came closer to an adequate doctrine of Scripture, yet Protestant rationalistic Orthodoxy of later centuries once more fell back into an increasingly docetic doctrine of Scripture. And under the devastating influence of Modernists, Fundamentalism retreated into a semi-docetic doctrine of the Word. Because Mennonites too read the literature of Fundamentalism, most of them were strong on the divine involvement of the Spirit of God in the production of the biblical books, but hardly aware that the Bible was also (paradoxically) a truly human book.

How Is the Bible Human?

First of all, the style of each writer is in evidence. John writes his Gospel as an old man, and employs the simple expressions of one who is old. The style of an old man seems even more evident in his epistles. Luke, by way of contrast, writes the prologue to his Gospel in classical Greek style, addressing his work to Theophilus and explaining his reasons and procedures for writing.

But this human element is more than a matter of style. Even the content reveals that in many passages the writer was allowed to record his fears, his doubts, and that which brought him back to faith in God. The psalmist, for example, in psalm 73 reports that the prosperity of the wicked greatly upset him. In good poetic style he embellishes this thought at some length: They have no pains. Their bodies are sound and healthy. They do not have the troubles that most people have. They are full of pride, and even of violence. They defy even God, and their tongue "struts through the earth." They claim that God is an absentee Deity as far as the earth is concerned! Only at verse 17 does the writer report where it was that his eyes of faith were really opened: It was when he went to the sanctuary of God that he was able to see the end of the wicked. Indeed, he saw that their destruction was imminent.

Perhaps the most striking thing in the whole picture is that God was able to come down to us and "lisp," as Calvin put it, in our limited human tongues. Our Indo-European languages have six tenses; Hebrew has but two. English has only two voices; Hebrew has seven, while Greek has three. Yet the Word of God can be translated into the various languages of earth, and still lead men to repentance and faith. Its effectiveness is not marred by the limitations of our several languages.

The Old Testament especially is Semitic in character—vivid, pictorial, concrete—and gives evidence that it is an ancient book. It delights in dialogue. How Abraham got a tomb for the body of Sarah is a good example. Today we would say that he purchased from Ephron the Hittite the field containing the cave of Machpelah for four hundred shekels. But the Hebrew records a delightful dialogue of the transaction.

The Bible abounds with round figures and the approximations of common people. Israel was in Egypt four hundred years. The stone jars of John 2 contained twenty or thirty gallons each. In John 6 the disciples rowed three or four miles.

The entire historiography of the biblical writers differs from ours. We carefully pinpoint events by calendar, clock, and geography. John Fitzgerald Kennedy was shot from the Texas Book Depository Building as he was in a car at the intersection of Houston and Elm streets a fraction of a second before 12:30 noon, Texas time, on Friday, November 22, 1963, supposedly by Lee Harvey Oswald. The Bible, however, does not date carefully and precisely even the birth of our Lord. We cannot be certain of date or month or even the year! The Bible is concerned more to tell us *what* happened, and the significance and *meaning* of the event. Modern historians also attempt to check their sources critically for the absoluteness of their accuracy. The Bible writers seem less sophisticated and more trustful of their sources.

One cannot state too emphatically that it was not the purpose of the Bible to anticipate modern learning. Today we know something of the size, mass, movement, and temperature of the sun and its family of tiny satellites. Scientists even know the process by which the sun converts 564 million tons of its mass into an end product of 560 tons of helium per second with a loss of four million tons per second which is released as heat. We know the orbits of the nine known planets with their scant three dozen moons. But none of this scientific data is in the Bible. The late astronomer, M. T. Brackbill of Eastern Mennonite College, was correct when he said: "The Bible was not written to tell us how the heavens go, but how to go to heaven."

The same humble silence applies to all of modern science. Today we still follow the basic lines of classification laid down in the eighteenth century by Karl von Linne (Linnaeus) of Sweden as set forth in his Latin monograph, *Systema Naturae* (1735). The Old Testament employs, of course, a far more ancient and simple classification: Wild animals, domesticated animals, those that fly, those that crawl, and those that live in the water—both the larger ones and "the lesser fry" as the commentator, Leupold, puts it. Leviticus 11:19 is therefore not in error in listing the bat with birds. It is in the pre-Linnaean class of creatures that fly.

I see no need of feverishly trying to prove that the Old Testament writers knew the exact numerical value of *pi* (what we call 3.14159265). They worked with the practical measurements of a builder, hence the diameter of Solomon's "Sea" in the temple was recorded as ten cubits across and thirty cubits around, not 31.416.

In parallel passages God allowed each writer to put down his observations and findings with a bland indifference to what others had written. A parallel would be a modern genealogist doing research in family history. He finds tombstone records as follows: Charles Smith (1807-92), his brother Henry Smith (1809-91), and then Jacob Smith (1811-98), and Isaac Smith (1811-96). He reports his findings in his book. Another researcher carefully points out that Jacob and Isaac were not twins as the readers of the book may have logically concluded, for he had found the family Bible records, and behold, Jacob was born January 3, 1811, and Isaac on December 17, 1811. Similarly, I see no reason to deny the slight apparent differences in the parallel passages of the Bible, for each is the true observation of an honest witness or researcher. For example, Peter evidently told the story of a certain person who declined to meet Christ's demand to give away his wealth (Mark 10). Matthew followed Mark's description ("a certain person") (19). But when Luke had interviewed his eyewitnesses, he was more specific. The "certain person" was "a certain ruler" (Luke 18). The gospels by their very diversities enrich our picture of the Savior! Furthermore, none of the accounts are full stenographic records of what was said; and so cold literary dissection can but distort the beauty of the tapestry which each evangelist has woven. And it must be remembered that Jesus taught in Aramaic, while the Gospels are written in Greek.

Higher criticism is a good and necessary study, but if the Bible is "God breathed" (2 Timothy 3:16) the assumptions with which one approaches it must be theistic and supernaturalist. For example, scholars such as Calvin were fully aware of the differences which appear in the Gospels without being unduly troubled by details which they did not know exactly how to fit together. Another biographical illustration may help. Samuel Jones and John Jones might be buried in the same row in the cemetery, and the stones might read 1857-1926 and 1858-1929. Yet some old man might insist that they were twins. The historical scholars discover that the medical records of the attending physician read that Samuel was born at three minutes before midnight, and John four minutes after midnight. The man of faith may hold to the full reliability of Scripture as a guide to faith and life while at the same time frankly acknowledging that he has a number of problems on the "waiting shelf" for which he has no easy answer. Those problems need call no article of the Christian faith into question—unless one has such a rigid view of inspiration as to deny the humanness of the Bible.

The competent Bible scholar acknowledges that the Masoretic text (Hebrew) of the Old Testament has a number of discrepancies as to numbers—seven hundred vs. seven thousand, for example. And when one compares the text of the Samaritan Pentateuch and that of the Septuagint (Greek) with that of the Masoretes, the discrepancies are even more numerous. But no blurring of the plan of salvation or of God's will for His children results.

The New Testament writers were so suffused with the glory of the Messiah Jesus that they often seized an Old Testament verse and applied it to Jesus, regardless of whether that passage was or was not obviously messianic in its original setting. The apostles were not concerned about "scientific" interpretation. They were persons who loved the Christ, and as they wrote or spoke, one passage after another which stated beautifully exactly what they wanted to say flashed into their minds. So they quoted them! This too is a part of the humanness of the Bible. But it in no way mars the witness of the apostles. It is true that Jesus is truly coming again, whether or not Jude actually knew who the Enoch was who spoke of His coming with ten thousands of His saints (verse 14). We must ever hold in tension that all the Bible is God breathed, and it is all human. We do not pounce with glee on a statement which shows the humanness of the writers of Scripture, nor are we "uptight" about problems we encounter. *As persons of faith we look for the truth which God in His goodness wants us to lay hold of.* "Open thou mine eyes, that I may behold wondrous things out of thy law."

Inspiration assures the believing reader that all Scripture is profitable for the end intended by the writer. Let us cling to the full authority of God's Word, the Holy Scriptures, when rightly measured against its stated purpose (2 Timothy 3:14-16).

It is possible to be too rigid in defining "truth" as scientific precision. One can be too troubled by apparent discrepancies in parallel narratives, the "scientific" accuracy of certain statements, or the relevance of certain statements for mathematics, history, or any field of learning. The Bible was not written to be a textbook of mathematics, science, history, astronomy, or any other field of human achievement. It was written to make us wise to salvation, to tell us how to believe in God, how to trust in Christ, and how to live a life of holy obedience to the precepts of God.

From Bishop George R. Brunk (1871-1938) I have learned that the Bible contains truth to be believed, a salvation to be received, experiences to be realized, warnings to be heeded, and promises to be claimed. In matters of salvation it is wholly reliable. In matters of this world it regularly employs "phenomenological" language, that is, events are described as honest witnesses observed them, not with the infinite precision that would be demanded of a scientist. It is my judgment that when rightly understood, and judged by what it intends to do, the Bible is wholly true, fully trustworthy, and inspired by God from beginning to end.

The Current Debate

When Modernism attacked the Bible on various fronts, the Fundamentalists tended to retreat to what they considered to be the safest possible asylum, that is, emphasis on the verbal and plenary inspiration of the Scriptures, seeing the Bible only as the Word of God. Rightly understood, that is good. But it is not the whole truth, and the entire truth needs to be stated if a totally true picture is to be portrayed. For the evidences of humanness appear on every page as we have seen. The position of the Reformers seems to me to be much more adequate, namely, that the Bible is fully trustworthy and authoritative *for faith and practice*. And this is the position of the best Evangelical scholars, for it centers on the central purpose of Scripture.

The debate over the meaning of inerrancy has surfaced again in Evangelicalism, and Harold Lindsell's book, *The Battle for the Bible*, states the case for a somewhat more narrowly defined inerrancy. It is difficult to see how he can deny that the Reformers understood the Scriptures' authority and trustworthiness as applying primarily to faith and practice. But apparently he must almost be pressed into a corner to admit it. While his statement of the authority of Scripture as the Word of God is laudable, by failing to point out its humanness sufficiently he does not provide a well-balanced doctrine of Scripture. Lindsell's motives are good and he has written a well-researched book with many fine points. But he seems all too ready to attack other Evangelical scholars whether or not they meant what he attacks them for. I fear that Lindsell's position is semi-docetic.

While Lindsell's book can be read with much profit by today's Christian believers, if one is to understand both sides of the debate, it is also necessary to read William Sanford LaSor's article in Fuller Seminary's *Theology, News and Notes* (Special Issue, 1976). The article is entitled "Life Under Tension—Fuller Theological Seminary and 'The Battle for the Bible.' "

We who wish to hold to the full authority of God's Word when rightly interpreted cannot but agree with the carefully worded *Westminster Confession of Faith* (1647):

> IV. The authority of the holy Scripture, for which it ought to be believed and obeyed, dependeth not upon the testimony of any man or church, but wholly upon God (who is truth itself), the Author thereof; and therefore it is to be received, because it is the Word of God.
>
> V. We may be moved and induced by the testimony of the

Church to an high and reverent esteem of the holy Scripture; and the heavenliness of the matter, the efficacy of the doctrine, the majesty of the style, the consent [Latin, *consensus*] of all the parts, the scope of the whole (which is to give all glory to God), the full discovery it makes of the only way of man's salvation, the many other incomparable excellencies, and the entire perfection thereof, are arguments whereby it doth abundantly evidence itself to be the Word of God; yet, notwithstanding, our full persuasion and assurance of the infallible truth, and the divine authority thereof, is from the inward work of the Holy Spirit [*ab interna operatione Spiritus Sancti*], bearing witness by and with the Word in our hearts."[9]

CHAPTER 7

Pop Eschatology: Hal Lindsey and Evangelical Theology

Marlin Jeschke

In a message to the 1971 Jerusalem Conference on Biblical Prophecy James M. Huston says, "I must ... confess that looking into the crystal ball has never been a hobby of mine. I have always felt that an exaggerated interest in the predictive element of prophecy often leads to unreliable, subjective views which, at their worst, tend to be schismatic, sectarian, and even on the lunatic fringe. We suffer enough scorn from the world for being Christians, my brethren, without suffering unnecessarily so from our own prophetic extravaganza."[1] These are feelings that I can echo, especially after once more going through the book *The Late Great Planet Earth* by Hal Lindsey.

In what follows we shall first review Lindsey, then attempt to set him in the context of Western eschatological thought in general, and finally critique his eschatology from the perspective of historic Mennonite theology.

Marlin Jeschke, professor of philosophy and religion at Goshen College, is the author of *Discipling the Brother* (Herald Press, 1972).

Lindsey Apocalyptic

In his opening chapter of *The Late Great Planet Earth*
Hal Lindsey draws attention to the popularity of astrology, futurology, spiritualism, and forecasting today.
The likes of Jeane Dixon reveal a hunger in people to
know the future. "We have clear and unmistakable signs
about the future," says Lindsey; "The Bible makes
fantastic claims; but these . . . are no more startling than
those of present-day astrologers, prophets and seers. . . .
We believe there is hope for the future. . . . A person can
be given a secure and yet exciting view of his destiny by
making an honest investigation of the tested truths of
biblical prophecy."

Lindsey then turns to a brief review of the Bible's
prophetic track record. The Old Testament makes numerous predictions that have been fulfilled. It predicted
judgment of Israel and Judah, the rise of world empires
such as Assyria and Babylon, the fall of Jerusalem, the
deportation of the Jews, and their restoration after
seventy years of exile. According to historic Christian
thought these predictions all came true. Furthermore the
Old Testament foretold the coming of the Messiah: His
birth in Bethlehem, His preaching in Galilee, His suffering and death on the cross, His burial and His resurrection. These prophecies of Micah, Psalm 22, and Isaiah 53
were also remarkably fulfilled. Again the Old Testament
predicted the regathering of Israel in the latter days from
the four corners of the world. This prophesy, says
Lindsey, we have seen fulfilled before our very eyes in
the Zionist movement and the establishment of the State
of Israel in 1948.

Given this proven reliability of Biblical prophecy,
Lindsey invites us to pursue further the quest for biblical

disclosures concerning the future. He finds first in Ezekiel's references (chapters 38 and 39) to Gog and Magog unmistakable identification of the latter-day power whose capital, Meshek, is Moscow, and whose prince or head (the Hebrew *Rosh*) is Russia. In Daniel 11 Lindsey espies a description of the Afro-Arabic confederacy led by Egypt. Egypt is Cush, the land to the south of Israel. But this Egyptian-led alliance is destined to fall by the sword (according to Ezekiel 30:4, 5) and will, in addition, suffer the national calamity of drought predicted in Isaiah 19:5, 6.

Yet another foe will attack Israel in the end time, "the Kings of the East." Revelation 16:12 "predicts the movement of a vast oriental army" from beyond the Euphrates "into a war in the Middle East." This Asian horde, numbering two hundred million (and Lindsey draws attention to the Maoist boast that China can muster a military force of two hundred million) "will wipe out a third of the earth's population" (Revelation 9:18). Lindsey sees Mao's China on schedule in its preparations to play its appointed role in the eschatological drama.

Then Lindsey sees in the ten-nation European Common Market the requisite revival of Rome called for by Daniel 7 and the reference to the ten horns of Revelation 13. The United States will need to suffer a decline in order to make possible a revival and dominating position for this ten-nation confederacy.

That brings us to the end of chapter eight and exactly half way through Lindsey's book. It brings us to the transition from past to future. Lindsey has sought to show what has already unfolded in conformity with prophecy; now he turns in the remainder of his book to what must yet appear. The drama's cast is, so to speak, poised for the closing act of world history.

The Antichrist is the next sign to be looked for in God's eschatological timetable. With Western civilization falling into political, social, and moral chaos, people will look for a dictator to rescue them. Lindsey here quotes with appreciation from Arnold Toynbee. "By forcing on mankind more and more lethal weapons, and at the same time making the world more and more interdependent economically, technology has brought mankind to such a degree of distress that we are ripe for the deifying of any new Caesar who might succeed in giving the world unity and peace." The Antichrist is the Beast of Revelation 13:1 rising up out of the sea. "He will have a magnetic personality," says Lindsey, "be personally attractive, and a powerful speaker. He will be able to mesmerize an audience with his oratory." (Lindsey offers no text to substantiate this characterization of the Antichrist.) The unmistakable sign of the Antichrist will be his recovery from a mortal wound to his head. Lindsey seems to be cautioning his readers against hasty identification of the Antichrist by counseling them to wait for the decisive revelation. Apparently the Antichrist has not yet appeared.

Accompanying the rise of Antichrist will be a parallel religious development, a false prophet and a false worldwide religion symbolically called Babylon. According to Lindsey we are already seeing the trend toward Babylon in the resurgence of astrology, in the "ecumaniac" movement, and in the drug culture. (The word for sorcery in Revelation 9:21 is from the Greek *"pharmakeia,"* which is behind our word "pharmacy." Thus he associates sorcery and the drug culture.) Lindsey throws these all together into one basket and predicts a false prophet who will lead the coming false religion in league with the Antichrist.

Then comes the "Ultimate Trip." When the world is about to blow up, Christ will return, says Lindsey, though only in the heavens to "rapture," that is transport, His saints. They will be caught up to meet the Lord in the air (1 Thessalonians 4:13-18), disappearing from the earth to the consternation of many people left here.

With this event, World War III is to be unleashed. Israel will accept the Antichrist's promise of protection, but Russia will invade from the North to precipitate Armageddon. By means of a couple of charts Lindsey takes us through the five phases of this final sequence of battles. Phase one sees a pan-Arabic assault on Israel. Phase two sees Russia counterattacking from the North (Daniel 11:40-42). Phase three marks the Russian conquest of Africa. Phase four finds the Russian commander hearing tidings of the mobilization of the Orient and of the Roman Confederacy, and so he regroups his forces. In Phase five the Russian army is destroyed in Israel. Revelation 14:20, which he associates with this battle, predicts a slaughter of such proportions that "blood will stand to the horses' bridles for a total distance of 200 miles northward and southward from Jerusalem" according to Lindsey (see p. 154).

The conflict will not be limited to the Middle East. All the cities of the nations will be destroyed (Revelation 19). "Imagine," says Lindsey, "cities such as London, Paris, New York, Tokyo, Los Angeles, Chicago obliterated." This judgment will finally bring the Jewish community to its senses. It will lead to "the greatest period of Jewish conversion to their true Messiah. . . ." At least one third of the Jewish community left on earth will accept Jesus Christ as Messiah.

Then comes the final event, Christ's sudden personal bodily return upon the Mount of Olives with His saints to judge the nations and to set up His millennial reign. Paradise will be restored. Carnivorous animals will change their nature. Satan will be bound. All people will submit to Christ's reign.

At the end of a thousand years of Christ's reign Satan will once more be loosed; there will be one final revolt against Christ by those whose submission was not genuine. This token rebellion will precipitate a final judgment, the creation of a new earth, the consignment of all the unrighteous to perdition, and the gathering of the saints into an eternal state of "righteousness, peace, security, harmony, and joy."

Here endeth the reading of Hal Lindsey. The eschatological scheme and genre will be familiar to many readers. A few preliminary comments are appropriate.

Lindsey represents the view of many Evangelicals. The two million copies of his book the publisher boasts having printed already in 1973 did not sell because of Lindsey's notoriety, or because of the literary merits of the book. It sold because a large number of people resonated with its message. We must note that Lindsey's eschatological thought is part of a larger pattern of biblical interpretation called dispensationalism. Lindsey himself is a product of Dallas Theological Seminary, which has for many years been a bastion of dispensationalist thought.

Lindsey does not, however, speak for all Evangelicals. This point is made rather forcefully by Clarence Bass and by numerous other theologians.[2] Moreover, the theory he represents is a latecomer upon the scene of theological history. Charles Ryrie in his defense of dispensationalism admits this indirectly when he claims that a given interpretation of Scripture is not necessarily false because it was not taught until the twentieth century.[3]

Lindsey in Historical Perspective

A review of millenarian thought in the history of Christianity in books such as Ernest Lee Tuveson, *Millenium and Utopia,* and Clark Garrett, *Respectable Folly,* show that Lindsey's eschatological scheme is only a brief and recent appearance in the kaleidoscopic succession of views that have succeeded each other through two thousand years of church history.[4] In order to put dispensationalism in its proper setting let us review this succession briefly. My review places Lindsey as the last in a series of seven eschatological views, a number and position I am sure he would appreciate.

1. The believers in all ages of the church have, of course, believed in a second advent of Christ. In the early church some of the church fathers expected a millennial reign of Christ in which the earth would be returned to paradisic glory. The church father Cyprian, for example, agreed with some of the Greek Stoic writers that the earth was getting tired and that it needed renewing. That is why crops were poor and why there were famines. Irenaeus expected this return of Christ to inaugurate a millennium of paradisic blessing when every vine would have 1,000 branches, every branch 1,000 twigs, every twig 1,000 clusters, and every cluster 1,000 grapes, each grape yielding 25 measures of wine.

2. By the time Augustine had written his *City of God* in the early fifth century this expectation of a future

millennial era had yielded to the view that the reign of
Christ was represented in the hearts of people rather
than in a future epoch. And with the growing power of
the Catholic Church after the fall of the Roman Empire,
the prevailing eschatological scheme identified the rule
of Christ with the church. Usually called triumphalism,
this view holds that with the Christianization of Europe
the kingdoms of this world had become the kingdoms of
our Lord, and His reign was expressed through His vicar,
the pope. With the coming of Christ Satan had been
bound.

This Augustinian eschatological view prevailed for the
longest period of church history. In fact, with the excep-
tion of people such as Joachim of Flora (d.1202) and Sa-
vonarola (1452-98) on the eve of the Reformation, this
medieval Catholic view prevailed for more or less a thousand years.

3. The Reformers modified the medieval Catholic eschatological scheme. They said that the first thousand
years of the church's history had indeed represented the
reign of Christ, but the beginning of the second millennium was marked by an apostatizing church and by a
degeneration of the papacy into the reign of Antichrist.
This charge that later popes represent not the reign of
Christ but of Antichrist will sound familiar to anyone
who has read Reformation literature to any extent. It was
a popular pattern of thought for some time, and it went
roughly as follows: The first 1,000 years of the church
represented the reign of Christ. Then came the reign of
the Antichrist, which was destined to last for 666 years.
That added up to the magic date of 1666, at which time
many people expected the end of history and of the
world.

If the evils of the church at the time of the Reformation were not enough, the Turkish Muslim invasions of Eastern Europe fulfilled the predictions of Revelation about vials of divine judgment and wrath. Remember that the siege of Vienna by Suleiman the Magnificent took place in 1529. That was when the Reformation was at its height! No wonder Luther expected the end of the world in his own lifetime. I think people like Lindsey owe it to themselves to reread some of Reformation history to get the feeling of how convinced European Protestants were of their experience as the fulfillment of the predictions of Revelation. The interpretation fit so perfectly, and the times of judgment were to them so real.

Let me quote from Tuveson's description of Luther's commentary on the Book of Revelation. At first Luther did not care much for Revelation because he thought it confusing and trivial. But in the course of time he changed his mind because he thought he saw a description of his own time.

> Chapters 7 and 8 of Revelation, for example, prophesy the coming of bad angels—that is, heretics. First is the doctrine of salvation through works; then Marcion, Manicheans, Origen, Novatian, Donatists, and others. After the first four angels there are the last three spirits of woe, compared with whom these earlier bodily and spiritual tribulations are almost a jest. Each of the three angels of tribulation is to be greater than his predecessor, and after the final one the present world is to end: Mohammed, the sixth one, is worse than the fifth, Arius; and as a grand finale, there is the 'strong angel with the rainbow and the bitter book,' that is, the papacy. . . . With chapter 14 of Revelation according to Luther's pattern, there begin a series of "comforts." The angel with the Gospel comes against the bitter book of the

strong angel. The second angel prophesies Babylon's fall and destruction—Babylon being the papacy. . . . In the interpretation of chapters 15 and 16 is a potent suggestion: the seven angels who pour out the seven vials of wrath symbolize the increase of the Gospel and the attacks on the throne of the beast (the papal power).

The significance of this new interpretation was very great. Luther succeeded in identifying Antichrist with a certain institution: the papacy. We are, therefore, he concluded, in the last days. His interpretation of the history of the City of God is optimistic, but otherwise he does not hold out much hope for the present world. The millennium is in the past; there is nothing for the true believers but to steel themselves for the steadily worsening blows to come, making sure that, whatever happens, they are not lured back into the fold of Antichrist. Thus by trials and persecutions the chosen people undergoes purification.[5]

4. The Reformation, almost contrary to the expectations of many Protestants, succeeded, especially in Protestant lands such as England, Holland, Switzerland, Sweden, and Germany. This led to a new interpretation of the *eschaton*. Instead of Armageddon and the end of the world in 1666 came the Puritan revolution in England, a turn of events that generated powerful hopes of a kingdom of God constituted by Calvinist legislation. John Milton, the great poet of Puritanism wrote in a spirit of "apocalyptic progressivism":

> . . . This great and Warlike Nation instructed and inur'd to the fervent and continual practice of *Truth* and *Righteousnesse*, and casting farre from her the *rags* of her old vices may press on hard to that *high* and *happy* emulation to be found the *soberest, wisest,* and *most Christian People* at that day when thou the Eternall and shortly-expected King shall open the Clouds to judge the severall Kingdomes of

the World, and distributing *Nationall Honours* and *Rewards* to Religious and just *Common-wealths,* shalt put an end to all Earthly Tyrannies, proclaiming thy universal and mild *Monarchy* through Heaven and Earth.[6]

The idea of the Fifth Monarchy, the reign of King Jesus, "had a tremendous, almost incalculable influence in these years of unrest" in England, says Tuveson. It was now held that the thousand years' binding of Satan had already begun with the Reformation. Notice the switch. Earlier, at the time of the Reformation, it was held that Christ's coming had bound Satan for 1,000 years, but then with the deterioration of the papacy Satan had been loosed. Now it was held that the successes of the Reformation marked the binding of Satan in order to permit Christ's rule to be established on earth for the *next* 1,000 years. This marks a 180 degree turn of thought. Yet the totally new turn of thought still found its rationalization in biblical prophecy. The Puritans believed that the four kingdoms past of Daniel's revelation bespoke the four monarchies of England, with the last one cut off in the Puritan revolution and the execution of King Charles I. The doors now stood open for the kingdom of our Lord and of His Christ.

5. The next eschatological scheme represents a softening of the one just sketched. The advances of science, of which the Puritans were in the vanguard, led to a modification of the hope of the millennial reign of Christ. More and more, thanks to technological and industrial progress, clergymen as well as scientists of the Royal Society (and very often they were both clergy and scientists) began to expect the blessing of the millennial reign of Christ to be ushered in through science, reason, and goodwill rather than through severe Calvinist legislation.

The thought is expressed very well by William Blake in his poem 'Milton'' published in 1804.

> I will not cease from mental fight,
> Nor shall my sword sleep in my hand,
> Till we have built Jerusalem
> In England's green and pleasant land.

Joseph Mede from an earlier time already anticipated this belief in progress. "According to Mede the progress of history since the time of Christ has been the gradual defeat of evil and the realization of the Gospel in human life." Note how a person sees through the glasses of a certain *Zeitgeist* (cultural perspective) and looks back at all of history through them. Mede no longer sees deterioration in the history of the church. He sees only progress.

This process is symbolized by the pouring out of the seven vials. The first represents the rising of the Albigensians and Waldensians; the second, poured out upon the sea (the compass of the Pope's jurisdiction), is the work of Luther and the reformers; the third, upon the rivers, must be the anti-Catholic laws of Elizabeth; the fourth is being realized in the Thirty Years' War, the fifth is to be the destruction of the Throne of the Beast, Rome itself; the last of these preparatory events is to be the conversion of the Israelites, accomplished somehow by destroying the Turkish power. The seventh will be nothing less than the final judgment, which is to coincide with the period of the millennium.

The last days before the culmination of history are, moreover, characterized by a remarkable enlightenment of mankind. ... [Mede finds in Daniel 12:4 a prophecy that the] 'opening of the world by Navigation and Commerce, and the increase of knowledge, should meet both in one

time, or age. ... And this increase of knowledge, which
these latter times have brought forth, appeares in nothing
more remarkeably, than in the interpretation of this mysterious booke, the Revelation of Saint John.'[8]

It may be hard for us to imagine, but Mede can read
the Revelation of St. John through the eyes of scientific
progress. He interprets the rising of the Lord in His glory
as the light of science.[9] Mede sees the Reformation as the
beginning of the dawn of the *eschaton.* "Not onely in
respect of the great Reformation wrought in this
Westerne part of the world an hundred yeeres agoe and
more: God awaking as it were out of a sleep, and like a
gyant refreshed with wine: and the Lord Christ awaking,
and stirring up his strength for the raising up of *Jacob,*
and restoring the desolations of *Israel.* ... "[10]

6. The French Revolution pushed European Christians into new patterns of interpretation of eschatology.
Especially Christians from the English tradition looked
across the channel with apprehension. They were filled
at first with hope but then with terror at the course of the
French Revolution. When at first the French king was
guillotined, the students of prophecy in England
believed they were observing the first of the ten kings of
Revelation dethroned, but with the reign of terror and
the rise of Napoleon these students of Bible prophecy felt
a grievous disappointment at the abortion of a promising
utopian era. Napoleon began to be looked upon as Antichrist.

7. Mention of Napoleon carries us into the beginning
of the nineteenth century and the rise of Dispensationalism in England, a school of thought that worked
out the eschatological views followed by Hal Lindsey.

It would be possible to make different classifications of eschatological schemes than the seven I have listed, but I have offered at least a sample of the historical variety of futurist expectations that people have seen in the Bible. (We have not, for example, looked at eschatological views of Russian Orthodoxy.) The review I have offered shows how variable and diverse these eschatological schemes are. One should note the tendency of people of every era to make biblical prophecy suit the current events of their time and to read especially Daniel, Ezekiel, and Revelation in accordance with their biased interests. I merely repeat the basic point: Lindsey's eschatology is a johnny-come-lately in the parade of Christian eschatologies, and to each holder of successive interpretations his own was convincing. None of us should minimize, for example, how seriously Reformation Christians took the pope to be the Antichrist.

Critique

Some commendatory and some critical things can be said about Lindsey's *Late Great Planet Earth*. The one basic point to be appreciated in Lindsey is his return, with most modern theology, from the theological wilderness of medieval allegorizing and of Protestant moralizing. In the Middle Ages, Jerusalem always stood for heaven. It could not be a place on earth. And in Protestant theology the promised land was peace within one's heart. It could not be a human community attempting to incarnate the rule of Christ in its institutions and corporate life.

The biblical message about a human community and a renewed earth is something that has been recovered after centuries of Hellenized Christian thought. The Christian faith does not speak about an escape to heaven; it does not speak about an abandonment of God's creation. From this perspective one could wish that Lindsey had entitled his book *The New Great Planet Earth* instead of *The Late Great Planet Earth*, for the Bible speaks of a re-creation of this planet in accordance with the original vision of God the Creator. Lindsey helps in some measure to reject Christianized versions of the platonic vision of the soul's return to its ethereal abode, although there is still too much of that left in his rapture idea.

Lindsey in this same vein helps us realize that there is genuine prophecy in biblical thought and biblical literature. Prophecy is not merely moral and social-ethical forthtelling, as liberal theology has tended to say, but is prediction. And these predictions can be tested. The prophets of the Old Testament were true or false according to the outcome of their predictions.

There are, however, also some shortcomings in Lindsey's book and in his view of the Christian hope. I will mention three.

1. Lindsey has a propensity, like many others, to read the Bible from an ego-temporal perspective, that is, to view the prophecies of the Bible, especially Daniel, Ezekiel, and the Revelation of St. John, as written directly for our age. As we have seen, the Christians of Reformation Europe thought that way too when they saw Vienna besieged by the Muslims. The Thirty Years' War was seen by its victims as one of the vials of divine wrath. The people of 1792 thought they were experiencing the fulfillment of Revelation when they saw the excesses of the French Revolution. And one "prophet" in London in 1795 predicted a giant earthquake for June 4 of that year. On that night a terrible rainstorm with

thunder and lightning descended upon London, and
many people fled the city, afraid it was indeed going to
be the end of the world.

And so it goes. First Mussolini is 666, then Hitler, then
Stalin, then Henry Kissinger. We read in Habbakuk
about chariots jostling in the streets, and conclude that
this must be a prediction of the automobile. We read in
Isaiah of doves flying to their windows, and see there the
prediction of the modern airplane. And when Peter's
epistle says the elements will melt with fervent heat, we
discern a prediction of the nuclear bomb. Such interpretations and applications are self-defeating, for
when one displaces and discredits the other it exposes
them all to be based on unreliable method.

As a footnote to this point it is ironic that Lindsey's
scheme provides no room for America in prophecy. The
only role that the United States has, according to
Lindsey, is to bow out, to become chaotic and weak, to
degenerate in a drug culture so that it can make way for
the United States of Europe. The reason, of course, is
very simple. At the time of Israel there was a Northern
power, Assyria, that threatened it, an Eastern power, and
a Southern power, Egypt. But to the West there was only
the Mediterranean. Therefore Israel's prophets never
spoke about a threat from the West. Perhaps if there had
been an important and developed navy at that time there
might have been a threat from the West. But, alas, since
there was no such threat, we in the USA have no role to
play in the final drama of Lindsey's eschatology!

2. There is a certain inconsistency and failure in
Lindsey to follow his own professed principle of the interpretation of Scripture. The basic principle of Evangelical interpretation of the Bible in general is *literal* in-

terpretation. We know, however, that it is not quite that simple. In one of his visions Daniel saw a bear, a lion, a leopard, and a goat. Are these to be taken literally? Of course not! Dispensationalism itself qualifies the "literal sense" rule to say that "literal" means the interpretation of words in the Bible in accord with the straightforward, ordinary, and general meaning they possess at the time a biblical document was written.

So far so good. All honest biblical scholarship attempts to uncover that meaning. But how do we find out what words meant at the time of their writing? Only by historical-critical scholarship, by finding out all we can about apocalyptic literature as a genre and of the historical context of the several books in particular.[11] Thus, for example, to understand the Book of *Revelation* we need some knowledge of what the Roman Empire was like, how it treated the Christians, how the Roman Empire symbolized itself, how Jewish apocalyptic literature symbolized the Roman Empire, and (from other literature besides Revelation, if possible) how Christians conceived of their situation at this time of persecution. But right here appears another historical question. What is the date for the writing of Revelation? When was Daniel written? Or Ezekiel?

For some literature of the Bible fixing the time of writing is not an acute problem. But in the case of the Book of Daniel for Lindsey to rule out the great consensus of biblical scholarship that Daniel is a document of the Maccabean era is immediately to disqualify himself as an interpreter of the straightforward literal meaning of Daniel. The Book of Daniel, (the stories of chapters 1-6 as well as the visions of chapters 7-12) addresses itself to the plight of Jews under Seleucid persecution ca. BC 165

(The Seleucids were Syrian kings who succeeded to a portion of the empire of Alexander the so-called Great.)

The inconsistencies of Lindsey on this point of straightforward literal interpretation may be shown thus: In the first chapters of his book Lindsey shows how prophets predicted the coming of Assyria, the fall of Samaria, the invasion of Babylon, the collapse of Jerusalem, the deportation, and the return. They also prophesied the coming of Messiah. And these prophecies were fulfilled, says Lindsey, as we have already noted. On these principles it is obvious that the prophecies of Ezekiel, of Daniel, of Jesus, and of John the Revelator were also fulfilled. The Holy Place was desecrated as the Book of Daniel says, and after "literally" 2,300 days (3 years and 2 months) it was purified and reconsecrated, an historic event celebrated to this day in the Jewish community as Hannukah, the festival of lights.[12] Jesus' prediction of the destruction of Jerusalem was also fulfilled in the Jewish-Roman war of AD 66-70, in which over one million people either starved, were killed, or were captured and sold into slavery. John's predictions of judgment upon the Roman imperial powers who persecuted the saints were fulfilled. His prediction of the vindication of the saints was fulfilled.

In all prophetic prediction—from the promise of God to Abraham that he would give him the land through Isaiah's vision of the peaceable kingdom to John's hope of a new Jerusalem—we must understand which "prophecies" have been fulfilled and which even today continue to represent an extension of Christian hope. Lindsey fails to distinguish carefully enough between specific predictions with their fulfillment and the general hope of a new creation and universal reign of Christ that persists in

Christianity still today as a future dimension. As a result he treats apocalyptic literature in the Bible too much like crystal ball prognostication.

One further observation on the "literal" interpretation of apocalyptic literature: if the fulfillment of past prophecy—the fall of Jerusalem, the deportation, restoration, and the coming of the Messiah—is a clue to future events, then Lindsey will need to scale down the dimensions of his expectations. Events, especially of a bad nature, always seem cataclysmic to those who experience them. But often the fulfillments that the Bible itself claims took place proved to be disconcertingly unpretentious, and less than awe-inspiring when they did take place. For example, the early church claimed that Jesus' coming to His hometown of Nazareth fulfilled the promise of the liberation of Galilee! (Luke 4:16-21). It claimed that the coming of the Holy Spirit at Pentecost fulfilled the Joel prediction that the sun would turn to darkness and the moon to blood before the great and terrible day of the Lord. Are these indeed fulfillments of Old Testament prophecies? Do these events show a "literal" reading of the Old Testament predictions on the part of the apostles? Were these the events that people expected?

There were so many preconceived stereotypes of the first advent of Christ that many people missed it when it came. Very possibly people today hold preconceptions about the *second* advent of Christ so tenaciously that if and when it appears the majority may again miss it.

3. I expressed appreciation for Lindsey's return from medieval allegory and Protestant moralizing to an interpretation that puts the Bible back into world history. This commendation must, however, be qualified with

the lament that dispensationalist eschatology is only a partial return. It is still stuck with the classic notion of two kingdoms that characterized classic Catholic and Protestant thought. The Middle Ages tried to fit the biblical doctrine of the reign of Christ into the framework of two kingdoms, an earthly and a heavenly. These two kingdoms were related so as to assure us that it was a qualitatively spiritual or heavenly reign of Christ, and yet really embodied and instituted on earth—by the use of the sword if need be. Thus we have the pattern of the pope and the Prince, the spiritual and the secular arms, the spiritual and the secular swords.

Dispensationalism follows the same theme, except that it alternates the earthly and the heavenly kingdoms. The Jews represent an earthly kingdom with the use of the sword, and the church represents a heavenly kingdom of the age of grace. Then the millennium represents the establishment of an earthly kingdom established by the sword, but once again the final heavenly kingdom will know only love and peace. The building blocks of dispensationalist eschatology come from the two-kingdoms doctrine of classic Catholic thought.

Dispensationalism seems to be unable, in other words, to envision a kingdom that puts the cross at the heart of structured human community. The cross is the means for the rescue of souls. The sword, violence, judgment, and coercion are inescapable means to an actual flesh-and-blood righteous human community. In dispensationalism the way of the cross rescues people *out* of the world. It is not finally the constitutive way of establishing the rule of Christ *in* the world. That can be done only by punishment and retribution, force and fear.

My criticism has been made again and again in Mennonite theology—in Guy Hershberger's *The Way of the Cross in Human Relations,* Norman Kraus's *Community of the Spirit,* and in John H. Yoder's *The Politics of Jesus.* Norman Kraus writes, "What has been attempted here is the . . . modest task of writing a prologue to the politics of *agape* . . . what has been criticized is . . . the failure of the church . . . to recognize the radically new character of *agape* and to acknowledge that it [agape] is indeed the standard for organizing the life and mission of the church."[13] That includes the love of the enemy and not the consignment of the enemy to destruction.

It is often said, of course, that Jesus came at first in lowliness and humility but will come again in power and glory. But was not His first coming also in power and glory? Did not the angels sing over Bethlehem? Did not Jesus say in John's gospel, "Glorify me with the glory which I had with thee before the world was"? John the evangelist explains his meaning: "Thus spake he concerning his cross." Perhaps the problem is not that Jesus' first coming was without glory so that the second coming will have to be in glory, but that we have missed the meaning of glory. The center of biblical faith is Jesus' cross and resurrection. The disciples were told, "This Jesus . . . will come in the same way as you saw him go into heaven" (Acts 1:11). It is the *crucified* Jesus, albeit risen, who will reappear. The second advent will be consonant with the first. He will come to finish what He began, not to repudiate what He began. No second coming of Christ will turn its back on the cross. The second coming of Christ is intended to achieve in human community the love, servanthood, compassion, meekness, and justice that was intended in the first advent of Christ to be the form of human existence. As Quakers have

reminded us, it is the Lamb that was slain who reigns
forever and ever. The cross is not the failure of the
kingdom, but the way to it and the mark of life in it.

The *Mennonite Encyclopedia* points out in its article
on "chiliasm" (the doctrine of a thousand-year reign of
Christ on earth following His second coming for His
saints) that "there is no trace of chiliasm in the first
generation of the main line of the Anabaptists, whether
Swiss, Dutch, or German, represented by such men as
Conrad Grebel, Michael Sattler, Hans Langenmantel,
Pilgrim Marpeck, Thomas von Imbroich, Obbe Philips,
Menno Simons, Dirk Philips, Leenaert Bouwens, and the
Hutterites Jakob Hutter and Peter Ridemann. From
many of these leaders we have tracts, books, or letters,
which more or less clearly delineate their doctrinal position, and none of these leaders exhibits chiliastic
views." [14]

The absence of such chiliastic thought is not fortui-
tous. Apocalyptic ideas pervaded the atmosphere at the
time of the Reformation, therefore millenarian teaching
is not missing by default.

The *Mennonite Encyclopedia* states that premillennial
views "made rapid progress in the (Old) Mennonite
group only after World War I. . . . In recent times premillennialism is receding somewhat. The church has
never officially recognized or adopted premillennialism,
except in two district conferences, whereas two district
conferences prohibit this teaching directly. Dispensationalism has never secured a hold in the group." [15]

The reason the Mennonite Church has declined to accept the eschatology of that Evangelicalism represented
by Lindsey is, to my thinking, simple and clear.
Anabaptist-Mennonite thought has taken seriously the

exaltation of *Jesus* as Lord and Christ. In the confession of His lordship it already recognized the coming of the kingdom of God. Consequently it has seen the church as the real, if anticipatory, embodiment of the reign of God already in the present.

Christ is enthroned. God has made Jesus both Lord and Christ (Acts 2:38). This reign of God through His appointed Son has not reached its consummation, to be sure. Nonetheless that reign is inaugurated and its form is the glory and triumph of crucified love.

CHAPTER 8

Evangelicalism and the
Mennonite Tradition

Ronald J. Sider

I want to work with two theses. First, if Evangelicals were consistent, they would be Anabaptists and Anabaptists would be Evangelicals. I will simply assert this statement without arguing at length.

Second, Mennonites need Evangelicals and Evangelicals need Mennonites. I will attempt to develop this thesis at greater length.

If they were consistent, Evangelicals would be Anabaptists and Anabaptists would be Evangelicals. Anabaptists have historically affirmed the central doctrines of the historic Christian creeds about which Evangelicals care a great deal such as the Trinity, the full humanity and full Deity of Jesus Christ, the atonement, and the bodily resurrection. Further, Anabaptists have historically had a central concern for evangelism. The Anabaptist missioners of the sixteenth century who

Ronald J. Sider is a professor at Eastern Baptist Seminary and Messiah College. A leader of Evangelicals for Social Action, he is the author of *Rich Christians in An Age of Hunger* (Inter-Varsity, 1977) and of *Christ and Violence* (Herald Press, 1979).

spread Anabaptist ideas all over Europe may be considered to be some of the earliest modern missionaries.

Finally, Anabaptists are committed to the full authority of the Scriptures as the norm for faith and practice. It was precisely their commitment to Scripture that led the early Anabaptists to challenge Zwingli and Luther. And it was the Scriptures which provided the foundation for that challenge.

Conversely Evangelicals, if they were consistent with their own commitment to biblical authority, would affirm emphases frequently associated with Anabaptism— an emphasis on costly discipleship, on living the Christian life, on the church as a new society living the ethics of the kingdom (and therefore living a set of values radically different from the world), on the way of the cross as the Christian approach to violence.

We Anabaptists have always insisted that we affirm these emphases because they are *biblical.* If they are biblical, then Evangelicals with their central concern for biblical authority ought to become "Anabaptist" at these points. If we really think, as I do, that our concern for costly discipleship, the new community, and nonviolence are biblical, then we ought persistently to ask Evangelicals how they can maintain their concern for *sola scriptura* without becoming "Anabaptist" at these points.[1] We should not, of course, be so insensitive that we formulate it in precisely those terms and demand that Evangelicals adopt the term Anabaptist! But we should insist that a strong emphasis on costly discipleship, the church, and nonviolence is not a special calling for Mennonites, but rather a necessity for anyone who wants a fully biblical theology.

My second thesis is that Mennonites need Evangelicals

and Evangelicals need Mennonites. I want to argue that in several ways.

In the first place, we need each other to avoid distortions of our common affirmation that the center of Christian faith is a personal living relationship with Jesus Christ. Mennonites and Evangelicals agree that in spite of the importance of creeds, liturgies, sacraments, and Christian community, the essence of Christian faith does not lie in careful affirmation of historic creeds, solemn participation in liturgies, sacraments, nor intense involvement in church structures (not even radical Anabaptist counter-communities). The essence of the Christian faith, as Menno, Zinzendorff, Wesley, and the great revival preachers all knew, is a personal, living relationship with the risen Lord Jesus; an individual I-Thou encounter with the One we together in community confess in the creeds and participate in in the sacraments.

Evangelicals and Mennonites need each other to correct distortions of this central affirmation. Evangelicals frequently appropriate this insight in an individualistic way that separates the personal relationship with the risen Jesus from the reality of the church as community. Evangelicals today need Mennonites to remind them that a living personal relationship with the risen Christ must include becoming a part of Christ's visible body, the new community; where all relationships are being redeemed; where all sinful divisions between races, classes, and sexes are being overcome; and where all the sisters and brothers together disciple and nurture each other until all grow up into mature personhood in Christ. Evangelicals, on the other hand, need to caution Mennonites that they dare not substitute anything else, whether an ethnic community identity or a concern to imitate Jesus' nonviolent way, for a living personal relationship with the Lord Jesus.

In the second place, Evangelicals and Mennonites need each other to maintain a balanced evangelistic concern. Evangelicals, quite rightly, stress the importance of the evangelistic mandate to spread the gospel to the more than two billion in our world who have never heard of Christ. The evangelistic task underlined so forcefully by the Berlin Congress on Evangelism and the Lausanne Congress on World Evangelization ought to be a more passionately urgent concern for more Mennonites. Too many Voluntary Service workers care a lot more about working for development and justice than they do about spreading the good news of forgiveness through the cross. Too many Mennonites hesitate to engage in verbal evangelistic proclamation and then hide behind the important truth that one significant way to announce the gospel is just to live the new community of Jesus' redeemed people. Mennonites need to be challenged by the vigorous evangelical concern for evangelism.

But Evangelicals also need Mennonites in order to develop a more holistic biblical gospel. The gospel announced by many Evangelicals is unbiblical in its individualism and heretical in its separation from a call to costly discipleship. According to the New Testament, the content of the gospel is not just individual forgiveness and regeneration. It is also the fact of the church and the lordship of Christ.[2] One important part of the good news we announce is that it is now possible to join Jesus' new society where all relationships (including economic relationships) are already being redeemed. The existence of this new peoplehood is part of the good news. Accepting the gospel is not just a vertical encounter with a justifying, regenerating God. It also involves new horizontal relationships because it involves entry into a new community where one studies the Word and works out the meaning of discipleship today in a body of brothers and sisters. Mennonites need to help Evangelicals correct the individualism of their evangelism.

In a similar fashion, Mennonites can help Evangelicals see how they have omitted costly discipleship from their evangelistic proclamation. The lordship of Christ is an essential part of the gospel we proclaim. And this Lord calls all His followers to costly discipleship. It is impossible to accept Jesus as Savior and persistently reject Him as Lord. Unfortunately evangelical evangelistic programs often place the emphasis so exclusively on forgiveness that they fall into a cheap grace that omits the costly demands of the gospel.

My second point, then, is that Evangelicals need Mennonites to help them rediscover the biblical teaching that our evangelism must emphasize the church and costly discipleship, and Mennonites need Evangelicals to help them recover their original passion for chattering the good news to everyone who will listen.

Third, Evangelicals need Mennonites to help them remember that from the biblical perspective orthopraxy (right living) is just as important as orthodoxy (right doctrine) and Mennonites need Evangelicals lest they forget that the converse is equally true.

One need not argue that in the last decades, at least, Evangelicals have both in practice and sometimes in principle made doctrine more important than ethics. Mennonites regularly make this charge against them, and they are right.

But since this is addressed to Mennonites, I want to concentrate on the other half of this point. There seems to be a tendency, at least among a few Mennonites, to make orthopraxis more important than orthodoxy. This emphasis is probably not true for the typical Mennonite congregation where the balance may still be one-sided in the same way that it is among Evangelicals generally. But there are signs here and there that a one-sidedness in the opposite direction would develop. There are some Mennonites who have demonstrated in their lives a very costly commitment to following the ethical teachings of Jesus and to living out the reality of the new society of Jesus' followers in intimate community who nonetheless seem to think that the historic Christian emphasis on the full deity of Jesus Christ and His bodily resurrection from the dead are dispensable doctrines. The essence of Christian faith is really the ethical life of following Jesus' teachings and the Sermon on the Mount is the canon within the canon.

Now neither of these distortions will do! We need the balanced stance of 1 John which says bluntly that any claim to know and love God which is divorced from active love for the hungry neighbor is a hypocritical lie. Mennonites need to remind Evangelicals just as vigorously as possible of this message of 1 John.

But Mennonites must not forget that the converse is equally true. It is precisely the same 1 John which insists just as pointedly that anyone who does not confess that Jesus the Messiah is the incarnate Son of God is the anti-Christ. If the early Christians had merely claimed that Jesus was a great prophet and moral teacher who preached a challenging Sermon on the Mount, they would never have broken with Judaism. According to

1 John, to deny that Jesus of Nazareth is the unique, incarnate Son of God is just as serious as failing to demonstrate our love for God by ignoring our needy neighbors. Orthodoxy and orthopraxy are equally important.

I want to develop this argument that we should be equally concerned with orthodoxy and orthopraxy by looking in more detail at two issues, the atonement and the resurrection.

Evangelicals frequently fail to appropriate the full biblical doctrine of the atonement because they fail to teach that Christians are to imitate Christ's way of dealing with His enemies in their own relationships with their enemies. On the other hand, Mennonites sometimes become so preoccupied with pacifism and nonviolence that they deemphasize the vertical aspects of the atonement.

As John Yoder has recently pointed out so vigorously, the New Testament repeatedly calls on Christians to imitate the way of suffering love revealed in the cross.

> There is thus but one realm in which the concept of imitation [of Jesus] holds—but there it holds in every strand of the New Testament literature ... this is at the point of the concrete social meaning of the cross in its relation to enmity and power. Servanthood replaces dominion, forgiveness absorbs hostility.[3]

In 1 Peter 2, Christian slaves facing unjust masters are urged to imitate the way of the cross; "For to this you have been called, because Christ also suffered for you, leaving you an example, that you should follow in his steps. ... When he was reviled, he did not revile in return; when he suffered, he did not threaten" (vv. 21-23). "Be imitators of God," Ephesians 5 says, "and walk in love, as Christ loved us and gave himself up for us, a fragrant offering and sacrifice to God" (vv. 1, 2). One could continue to cite illustrations (Luke 14:27-33; Mark 10:43-45; 1 John 3:11-18; 4:7-12). But the point is clear. The New Testament explicitly and repeatedly commands Christians to love their enemies in the nonviolent, self-sacrificing fashion of the crucified Jesus.

If we Evangelicals really believe as we claim that Jesus is Lord and that canonical Scripture is fully binding, then surely there is only one possibility. If Scripture calls us to love our enemies the way Jesus loved His enemies at the cross, we must either accept the way of nonviolence or abandon our proudly proclaimed principle of scriptural authority. Because the way Jesus atoned for our sins was to carry love for the enemy to the ultimate degree, a refusal to obey His command to follow His example at this point not only involves a denial of scriptural authority; it also constitutes a heretical doctrine of the atonement. God chose to reconcile His enemies and accomplish the atonement by nonviolent, suffering love. If we reject the biblical imperative to follow Jesus at precisely this point, we in effect express disbelief about the validity or effectiveness of God's way of reconciling enemies. But to do that is to express disbelief about the atonement itself which Jesus accomplished by loving His enemies.

On the other hand, there is another equally serious heresy of the atonement that relates to our topic of nonviolence. Some pacifists seem inclined to reduce the doctrine of the atonement to a revelation of God's method of dealing with evil. According to one Anglican writer in a collection of essays edited by the Quaker pacifist Rufus H. Jones, the cross is "Christ's witness to the weakness and folly of the sword. . . . Jesus is acknowledged as the Saviour precisely because He challenged and overthrew man's reliance upon military power."[4]

We need not believe that St. Anselm's *Cur Deus Homo* is verbally inerrant in the original autographs, that the penal substitutionary view of the atonement is correct at all points, or that by itself it captures the fullness of the biblical view of the cross. As Leon Morris noted recently in *Christianity Today,* "No theory is adequate. . . . We need the contributions of quite a few theories to express something of what the Cross meant to the men [sic] of the New Testament."[5] Certainly the moral view of the atonement does express one important part of the New Testament teaching on the cross. But to reduce the meaning of the cross either to a revelation of the validity of pacifism or, with Abelard, to a powerful disclosure that God is love, is simply unbiblical.

The New Testament asserts not only that sinful persons are hostile to God, but also, and with equal clarity, that the just Creator hates sin. Paul reminded the Romans that "the wrath of God is revealed from heaven against all ungodliness and wickedness" (Romans 1:18). For those who know the law, failure to obey it results in a curse. But Christ redeemed us from that curse by becoming a curse for us (Galatians 3:10-14). Jesus' blood is an expiation (Romans 3:25; 1 John 4:10) and the result is unmerited acquittal (Romans 5:18) for sinners precisely because the One who knew no sin was made sin for us on the cross (2 Corinthians 5:21). A pacifism which belittles or ignores this aspect of the cross will not find a welcome hearing among evangelical Christians. And it should not, because it is not biblical.

I sense a vastly less serious but related problem in John

Yoder's discussion of justification in *The Politics of Jesus*.[6] Yoder explicitly says that in developing the social dimensions of the concept of *dikaisune* (righteousness) he is not denying the personal side.[7] But then he proceeds to develop his argument and interpret the passages in a way that belittles the central role of forensic justification in Pauline thought. This is a mistake both exegetically and strategically. Precisely the central Pauline doctrine of forensic justification, which presupposes the kind of understanding of the atonement outlined above, is the basis of that new peoplehood of God which is called to be God's instrument of reconciliation and a living model of nonviolent peacemaking.

Ephesians 2 is the classic passage.

But now in Christ Jesus you who once were far off have been brought near in the blood of Christ. For he is our peace, who has made us both one, and has broken down the dividing wall of hostility, by abolishing in his flesh the law of commandments and ordinances, that he might create in himself one new man in place of the two, so making peace, and might reconcile us both to God in one body through the cross, thereby bringing the hostility to an end (Ephesians 2:13-16).

The crucial question is: Who is hostile toward whom? Yoder argues that the "hostility brought to an end in Christ is first and foremost in this passage not the hostility between a righteous God and man who has transgressed against His rules, but the hostility between Jew and Greek."[8] But there would seem to be no basis in the text for Yoder's preference. Verse 12 indicates that before they became believers, the Gentiles were both separated from the people of God (Israel) and also alienated from God, i.e., they were hostile both to the Jews and to God. Kittel's dictionary suggests that the hostility in this passage is twofold:

> We hardly do justice to the passage if we do not perceive that the Law plays a double role, dividing the Gentiles from the commonwealth of Israel and also Israel from God. By the Law there arises both the enmity between Jews and Gentiles and also that of man towards God. ... When Christ abolished the Law, He set aside the twofold disorder of the race both among men and toward God.[9]

I would argue in fact that we must see the hostility here as threefold. Certainly Jews were hostile to Gentiles, and all sinners are hostile to God. But in light of our previous discussion of God's wrath against sin, we must add that this passage refers also to God's hostility to sin.

And it is precisely the cross that ends the hostility and brings peace. Central to Pauline thought is the view that the cross makes possible a new kind of righteousness before God based not on observance of law and commandment but rather on faith (e.g., Philippians 3:2-11). Precisely because the crucified Jesus became sin for us, we have peace with God. "Imputed" righteous is reckoned to us. As Paul says in Romans right after a careful statement of forensic justification, it is "since we are justified by faith [that] we have *peace* with God.[10] Thus, precisely, this vertical peace with God, this imputed forensic justification is the basis of the new social peace in the body of believers. Because Jews and Gentiles are accepted before God on precisely the same basis, namely faith in Christ's cross, they now share a radically new equality.

Because all—Jews, Gentiles, slaves, masters, women—

are justified by faith alone, they are one in a radically new way. And the early church, of course, incarnated this doctrinal assertion in her common life by offering to the world a visible new community where all society's hostile dividing walls had already been broken down. Rather than seeing the forensic and social aspects of the Pauline doctrine of justification as competing emphases, we should see them as inseparably interrelated and complementary. Forensic justification is the foundation for the new reconciled and reconciling community.

Other passages support this interpretation. In Romans 3, Paul states most pointedly that since all people have sinned, their only hope for salvation is justification by grace through faith in the expiation effected through Christ's blood on the cross (vv. 24, 25). But then Paul proceeds immediately to the thesis that Jews and Gentiles are of equal concern to God precisely because He justifies both by faith alone (vv. 27-31).

Similarly in Acts 10, Peter announces to Cornelius that he brings the gospel of peace and then proceeds to show that everyone (even Gentiles) who believes in Jesus receives forgiveness of sins. The gospel is a gospel of peace precisely because it reconciles hostile racial, cultural, and sexual groups when they realize that they all receive forgiveness on exactly the same basis.[11] And at Antioch, Paul rebuked Peter for his refusal to eat with Gentile Christians by appealing to the doctrine of justification by faith. It is precisely because both Jews and Gentiles are justified by faith rather than works of law that Peter dare not separate himself from brothers and sisters (Galatians 2, especially verses 14-16).

To summarize, we should not stress the important social dimensions of the Pauline concept of righteousness in such a way that we overlook the central forensic element in the Pauline doctrine. And we should not stress the way of the cross as Jesus' new way to approach the tragedy of war and violence and overlook the fact that at the cross Jesus also bore the curse which our sins deserved.

A similar argument can be made for the relation of Jesus' resurrection and the doctrine of nonviolence. The bodily resurrection of Jesus is not just an esoteric theological doctrine which Evangelicals can use to ferret out liberal theology. It is the foundation of our radical discipleship today.[12] Because the resurrection demonstrated that the Carpenter from Nazareth is Lord of the universe, we can defy all other would-be lords (including presidents, generals, and dictators) for the sake of justice for the oppressed. Because the risen Lord is lord of the dead and the living, we dare to risk even death itself to seek liberation for the poor.

The resurrection of Jesus is also directly relevant to our Mennonite concern for nonviolence. Nonviolent movements often disintegrate when they experience the full force of organized injustice and systemic evil. Jesus' resurrection provides a solid anchor for our nonviolence. The knowledge that Jesus experienced all the evil that the fallen principalities and powers could inflict and nevertheless conquered them in His resurrection will steady our commitment.

But precisely at this point, a blunt candid question forces itself upon us: Will just *any* understanding of the resurrection be an adequate foundation for our hope? In his powerful book, *The Nonviolent Cross*, James Douglass makes a great deal of the resurrection. However, for him the resurrection is only a symbol of oppressed people awakening to the power of nonviolence.

> For it is true of the suffering poor who fill the earth that
> there is God in these people, like the fire that smolders
> under the ashes. There is no God other than the fire under
> these ashes. If God appears dead in the Nuclear Age, it is
> because He has not been sufficiently liberated from His
> bondage in suffering man. ... God lives where men are
> beaten and die, but He lives to bring them and their
> murderers to life, and His life comes to life *only* when He
> emerges from them as Truth and as Love. The life of God is
> the life of the crucified, but while He is deeply present in
> crucifixion, the unveiling of His presence is in resurrection,
> a resurrection that can be seen and felt only by those in
> whom Love and Truth have taken hold. ... Crucifixion be-
> comes redemptive precisely when the victim recognizes his
> [man's] divinity. Man takes that step when he responds to
> injustice with Love.... Man becomes God when Love and
> Truth enter into man, not by man's power but by raising
> him to Power, so that revolution in love is revealed finally as
> the Power of resurrection.[13]

Gordon Kaufman, professor at Harvard Divinity
School, provides another illustration. According to
Kaufman, the resurrection is the foundation of a new
movement of love and peace even though it was really
only a "series of hallucinations!" Writes Kaufman, "On
one level we can say that these alleged appearances were
in fact a series of hallucinations produced by the wishful
thinking of Jesus' former disciples."[14] Hence modern
people need not believe that Jesus was alive on the third
day. "Contemporary belief, of course, will not necessarily involve the conviction that the crucified Jesus became personally alive again; rather it will see the events
of Jesus' ministry and death—especially as appropriated
through that strange event called the 'resurrection'—as

the actual establishment of the kingdom of God . . . the founding of a new community of love. . . . "[15]

Such views are both unbiblical and inadequate. If by Jesus' resurrection we mean merely the birth of nonviolent convictions or the inner assurance of the early church that they should continue to follow the way of love taught by the Nazarene, then our hope is based on nothing more than our own subjectivity. Our hope will be as weak as our feelings. As Paul argued in 1 Corinthians 15, if Jesus of Nazareth has not been raised from the tomb, then Christian faith is useless.

Such an assertion raises a fistful of knotty philosophical and methodological problems for modern secular people. Although I cannot do it here, I believe these questions can be answered.[16] As a historian, I think one can say that there is surprisingly good historical evidence for the early Christian announcement that the tomb was empty and that they had seen and talked with the resurrected Jesus of Nazareth. And I think that fact stands as a powerful external sign which establishes and confirms our belief and hope that because Jesus has been raised from the dead, evil, violence, and death are ultimately fragile and weak.

John Updike puts it well in a recent poem:

> Make no mistake: if He rose at all
> it was as His body.
> It was not as the flowers
> each soft Spring recurrent;
> it was not as His spirit in the mouths and
> fuddled eyes of the eleven apostles;
> it was as His flesh: ours.
> Let us not mock God with metaphor,
> analogy, sidestepping, transcendence;

> making of the event a parable, a sign
> painted in the faded credulity of earlier
> ages:
> let us walk through the door.[17]

We dare not become so preoccupied with our crucial concern for nonviolence that we think the New Testament understanding of the resurrection is a dispensable notion which we can safely jettison without losing the essence of Christian faith. If Jesus of Nazareth did not rise from the tomb, then our faith is in vain and the foundation for our courageous commitment to the nonviolent way is lost.

The Mennonites' and Evangelicals' emphases on ethics and doctrine balance and complement each other. If, on the one hand, some Mennonites tend to make ethics the center and essence of Christian faith, Evangelicals, on the other hand, tend to belittle the importance of costly discipleship. Both positions may lead to serious distortion of the biblical perspective. Orthodoxy and orthopraxy are equally important.

My fourth and final point is that Mennonites need Evangelicals because a large number of Mennonites[18] are in danger of losing their own historic Mennonite concern for simplicity, costly discipleship, and identification with the poor. By Evangelicals at this point, I mean the radical Evangelicals represented by journals like *Sojourners* and *The Other Side*.

These people have learned a great deal from Mennonite authors about costly discipleship, concern for the poor, and the church as a counter-community living by a set of values different from the rest of society. In fact, these radical Evangelicals have learned what a large number of Mennonites seem to be in a rush to forget.

If Mennonite congregations at one time were way ahead of other Evangelicals in their commitment to costly discipleship, the church as community, and concern for the poor, it no longer seems to be true that there are many more Mennonites than other Evangelicals who really demonstrate by their lives that God is on the side of the poor.

Mennonites, along with Evangelicals in general, have fallen into a theological liberalism at this point. We usually think of theological liberalism in connection with issues like the bodily resurrection and the deity of Jesus Christ. And that is correct. Theological liberals have fallen into serious heresy in recent times by rejecting those basic doctrines of historic Christianity. But notice why that happened. Modern people became so impressed with modern science that they thought they could no longer believe in the miraculous. So they discarded the supernatural aspects of Christianity and abandoned the resurrection and the divinity of Christ. They allowed the values of surrounding society rather than biblical truth to shape their thinking and acting. That is the essence of theological liberalism.

In our time we are in great danger of repeating exactly the same mistake, that is, of allowing surrounding society rather than Scripture to shape our values and life in the ethical area of justice for the poor. Even though the Bible says as much about this set of issues as it does about the atonement or Christology, our economic values, our economic lifestyles, and our attitudes toward the poor have been shaped more by an affluent materialistic society than by the Bible.

If we want to escape theological liberalism, if our confession that Jesus is Lord is genuine, then we must cast aside the secular economic values of our materialistic society. Many of the people in our churches do not want to do that. They do not want to hear the Bible's radical call to costly discipleship. But that simply raises in a more painful way for every church leader the basic question: Is Jesus really my Lord?

Unfortunately, there are too many Mennonite and Brethren in Christ pastors, Sunday School superintendents, and other church leaders who agree that we should be concerned with the poor and work for peace with justice, but they are willing to talk about these things only so long as the message is not too upsetting to the congregation, so long as it does not offend potential new members and hinder church growth. They do not make it clear, as Jesus did, that we really must choose between Jesus and Mammon. They are afraid to teach and preach the clear biblical word that economic systems perpetrate institutionalized violence and murder because that would offend business people. I sometimes wonder whether it is Jesus or church growth, whether it is Jesus or vocational security, whether it is Jesus or social acceptance who finally is our Lord.

Few church traditions are as helpful as the Mennonite tradition for enabling us to understand and live out the biblical teaching that God is on the side of the poor. Simplicity in both personal lifestyles and church life has been a part of our heritage for centuries. We of all people ought to be able to hear the God of the poor calling us today to more simple lifestyles. But one only needs to look at the incredible wealth and affluent lifestyles among our people to see that this generation is abandoning that heritage at a fantastically rapid pace. Our parents and grandparents still understood the basic biblical call for separation from the sinful materialistic values of surrounding society even though at times they applied it in a superficial legalistic way. Will there by any heritage of simplicity left to pass on to our children?

The following story illustrates the problem. Last summer a Presbyterian couple I know came to a "Families for Justice" retreat. During the weekend, they shared their agonizing difficulty in communicating their concern for a simple lifestyle with their teenage son. They pointed out that he went to a Christian high school where all his friends had their own cars with nicely remodeled interiors and cassette players. Naturally he wanted a car for himself. Each family drove two or three cars to church on Sunday. Rather than helping them to communicate biblical values to their son, the Christian high school, and even the church, was subtly instilling the materialistic, sinful values of surrounding society.

Then the couple explained that their son was attending a Mennonite high school. They explained that they had left another Protestant church and joined the Mennonites in order to find support for their commitment to simple living. To their dismay, they discovered that most of the Mennonites there were moving rapidly in the other direction.

My final point then is that Mennonites need radical Evangelicals to help them keep from losing and in some cases begin to recover their own Anabaptist heritage.

I have argued two theses. First, consistent Evangelicals are "Anabaptist" in their concerns and consistent Anabaptists are Evangelical. Second, Mennonites need Evangelicals and Evangelicals need Mennonites. If these two theses are valid, there ought to be considerably increased interaction at all levels. At this point in time, the loosely knit groupings designated by the label Evangelical are in a period of rapid transition. There is unusual openness to historic Anabaptist concerns. My hope is that Mennonites will seize this opportunity to help shape the larger evangelical body. But it is crucial that they do so in such a way that they redisover and reaffirm rather than lose their own unique heritage of radical discipleship.

CHAPTER 9

Anabaptism and Evangelicalism

C. Norman Kraus

In order to compare and contrast Anabaptism and Evangelicalism one must first define the two movements, and that in itself is by no means an easy task. Both movements are diverse. Indeed, that is at least one thing they have in common. Anabaptism is a sixteenth-century European movement while Evangelicalism is a twentieth-century American movement. The cultural and historical contexts are significantly different, so what belief patterns and characteristics shall be used in the comparison? And to complicate the matter Anabaptism has been given a wide variety of interpretations. Which model of Anabaptism shall we use?

Heinrich Bullinger, who succeeded Ulrich Zwingli as pastor in Zurich, pictures the Anabaptists as revolutionary radicals who were intent upon upsetting all major social institutions and moral foundations of society. He interpreted their nonresistance and nonswearing of oaths

---

C. Norman Kraus is professor of religion and director of the Center for Discipleship at Goshen College. His most recent book is *The Authentic Witness* (Eerdmans, 1979).

as a lack of patriotism and support of the Christian government. And their refusal to baptize their children, a sign of their identity with the Christian social-politcal order, implied a radical rejection of both the church and state. The Hutterite espousal of community of goods inspired many of the same fears that communism raises today; and the few cases where some extreme Anabaptists advocated polygamy plus what seemed to Bullinger a general advocacy of anarchy convinced him that they were intent on destroying the traditional institution of marriage. In short, they advocated polygamy, communism, and sedition according to Bullinger, and they were willing to resort to violence in order to gain their ends. All of this, he claimed, was based upon the wild claims that they had direct revelations from God which nullified biblical and theological authority.

At the opposite end of the interpretative continuum stands the modern Mennonite historian, John Horsch, who played an important role in the renaissance of Anabaptist studies. Horsch was deeply involved in the Fundamentalist-Liberal debate at the same time that he was writing Anabaptist history, and he attempted to make Anabaptism fit the canons of Fundamentalism. For example, he published a two-part article in the *Gospel Herald* (July 1910) made up of quotations from Menno Simons to demonstrate that "early Mennonites were not unorthodox in their teaching on the authority of the Scriptures," and that they considered creeds and doctrine as important as other contemporary denominations. According to Horsch Anabaptists were strictly biblicists and thoroughly orthodox in their theology.

In between these two extremes are a number of models current today which interpret the sixteenth century after the patterns of the twentieth and view the Anabaptists as the first believers church denomination. This interpretation was developed as Mennonitism began to emerge on the American church scene as a recognized denomination. Anabaptism was pictured as a movement intent on forming a network of disciplined congregations under a secular government. It was based on biblical authority, conservative in its theology, completely nonviolent, and cooperative with government insofar as conscience allowed. It emphasized individual conversion and discipleship. Thus it was pictured as the prototype of a free church.

Then in the turbulent late sixties a new image of Anabaptists was introduced which Art Gish spelled out in *The New Left and Christian Radicalism.* Anabaptists were the radical (going to the root) followers of Jesus challenging the establishment. They were demanding a new order of social-economic structures based upon a counterculture model. Menno, as well as the Hutterite Ridemann, was quoted as highly critical of developing capitalism. "They were early socialists" so far as community ideals were concerned.[1] Denck, Grebel, and the rest stressed no compromise and noncooperation with self-serving religious and political institutions. They favored radical freedom to the point of anarchism. In short, according to this interpretation, these left-wing Christians were agents of social change through simply being radically nonconformed and obedient to the lordship of Christ. They accepted the New Testament, and especially the Sermon on the Mount, as a blueprint for setting up communities of obedience. Thus the revolution was to be completely nonviolent based on *agape* and radical self-denial.

One could multiply these interpretative models almost endlessly, but there is one more that has particular significance since we are considering comparisons with Evangelicalism. It is a model that implicitly has been based on patterns which developed in the "New Evangelicalism." According to this interpretation, Anabaptists were above all engaged in a great evangelistic revival of personal, biblical religion. Their emphasis was upon voluntary personal commitment and conversion of the individual; upon the Bible as a practical guide for life and the primary call to individual witness. They provide the early prototypes for *koinonia* groups in which community is defined in terms of primary social relationships.

Obviously, the model of Anabaptism one uses to compare with Evangelicalism will influence the comparison decisively. And just as obviously no model of Anabaptism or Evangelicalism will be entirely objective. There are elements of historical fact in each of the above models. What we must try to avoid is self-justification and self-serving in our descriptions and comparisons. As much as possible at this point it will be helpful to stand back from both movements and learn from them by juxtaposing and evaluating them. There are clear differences between them, and according to both the Scriptures should provide the criterion for a final evaluation.

An Anabaptist Model

As we have noted, each of the above models has some elements of historicity in it, but each of them, except Bullinger's, already implies a comparison because each has used a modern paradigm to interpret Anabaptism. Such a comparison will also be implicit in any descriptive model that I suggest, but I think that it is possible to give a description that is both fair to the historical movement and provides a basis for evaluative comparison and contrast with modern Evangelicalism from several angles.

The Anabaptist movement may be characterized by four words. It was a *radical, Jesus-centered, martyr movement*. It was *radical* in the sense that it called for fundamental change not only of the individual but of the social order. It offered a radically prophetic critique of both the church and society of its day. It did not call for a revival or reform but for a re-creation. The Anabaptists were convinced that the old church was false, not just carnal; that its stance as a buttress of the "Christian social order" had involved it in a self-contradictory compromise.

Further, Anabaptists were radical in the sense that they called for immediate action. They insisted on obedience now in contrast to Zwingli who taught and urged obedience but would not move ahead of the council to initiate action.

Anabaptism as a whole was *Jesus-centered* rather than Bible centered. As central as the Bible was for them it remained a tool, a witness to Jesus Christ and not an end in itself. It was not so much a sacred book of revealed theology as an inspired witness to Jesus Christ. Thus they were not primarily concerned about theories of inspiration and inerrancy. Rather they accepted it as an authentic reflection of Jesus and asked what it would mean to obey it. They assumed its authority because they took for granted that it was an accurate report of Jesus' ministry and teaching. Menno held, for example, that the apostles' message had authority because it was the teaching they received from Jesus. By the same token they tended to give more emphasis to the Gospels than to the epistles.

Third, Anabaptism was a *martyr* movement. Martyr means witness, and the Anabaptists were the original evangelists of the Reformation. The principle of voluntary commitment required a dynamic witness and recruitment for the recreated church of Jesus Christ. Franklin Littell has pointed out that the original Hutterite communal organization was actually a missionary economic strategy.

But they were more than evangelists. They were martyrs. They lived out what they proclaimed. "No one," said Hans Denck, "can know Christ unless he follow Him in life." Theirs was a witness of demonstration in both individual and community lifestyle. It was this holistic, uncompromising witness which Menno called "bearing the heavy cross of Christ," and "giving a bold confession," and he gave these as identifying marks of the true church.

Last, Anabaptism was a *movement*. Often the term sectarian is applied to it, but that is in many ways a misnomer for the first generation of Anabaptist witness. They were not interested in a separate, sectarian church. Their goal in the first instance was to change the larger social order. They engaged in broad theological debate. They gave a political witness; and, as we have seen, they were aggressively evangelistic. Their strategy of confrontation and noncooperation with an evil system was a fundamental part of their witness for change. It was in no sense withdrawal from concern and responsibility. They were what Orlando Costas calls "prophet-evangelists."

The Mennonite descendants of the Anabaptists have often overlooked this last point. The sectarian compromise of the Anabaptist movement took place in the second and third generations in the face of severe persecution. And even then such issues as voluntary baptism, nonswearing of oaths, and nonresistance were clearly political as well as religious. Their sectarian witness continued to have a public and political relevance that sectarianism in America no longer has.

Contemporary Evangelicalism

By virtue of historical circumstance contemporary Evangelicalism has many dissimilarities with sixteenth-century Anabaptism. It also has a different theological and sociopolitical tradition that make it self-consciously different at strategic points. On the other hand, insofar as the principles of voluntaryism and separation of church and state have informed Evangelical theology and practice it shares some characteristics which classical Protestantism did not. For example, Evangelicalism shares a measure of commonality with Anabaptism in its emphasis from Pietism upon personal religious experience and the need for commitment; its insistence upon the centrality of witness and mission; its growing concern for a holistic gospel which speaks to the whole of human life; and its concern for the larger social order—although as we shall see, this is a qualified similarity.

If, however, we are to make more precise and detailed comparisons, we will have to ask which segment or interpretation of Evangelicalism is being compared. In what follows I propose to take several descriptive models for comparison and contrast at different points.

If we interpret contemporary Evangelicalism as neo-

Fundamentalism, or what Quebedeaux called "Establishment Evangelicalism,"[2] there is perhaps more contrast than comparison. From this perspective its characteristics are clearly those of a second-generation stage in the social evolution from the Fundamentalism of the 1920s and 1930s. The movement is from minority to majority psychological status with adjustments in living standards to its growing affluence and political power. At this point Establishment Evangelicalism enjoys without a scruple a new social-political acceptance which approaches a reestablishment of it as the dominant civil religion.

In this guise it is the defender of "the American way of life" and an ally of the Pentagon. It is an aggressive promoter of the West's nineteenth-century imperialistic missionary conquest. It is pragmatic in its use of means and makes deliberate use of advertizing and marketing techniques and of mass media to spread the message. In contrast to an earlier Fundamentalism which eschewed the mixing of politics and religion, it aggressively uses its political clout to bring about moral and religious reform through law. Its theology is essentially fundamentalistic with modifications that are more in mood and tone than in substance. It is more tolerant of difference within evangelical limits, and more willing to cooperate in achieving its ends. Its message is positive, success oriented, encouraging self-initiative, and promising individual fulfillment and security in spite of a discouraging prospect for society at large.

While this is not a complete and balanced description of the movement, it is an accurate analysis of its dominant sociological characteristics. And viewed from this perspective it has almost nothing in common with

Anabaptism. Rather, it smacks of a revival of an older puritan domination.

Revival of Classical Protestant Theology

If we interpret Evangelicalism as a revival of classical Protestant theology freed from the negativism and defensiveness of earlier Fundamentalism as, for example, Bernard Ramm and Kenneth Kanzer do,[3] then a different assessment and comparison is needed. We are dealing here with a theological rather than a sociological view, and the elements for comparison are more complex.

According to this interpretation Evangelicalism stands directly in the heritage of the Reformation, and it represents the renewal of theology and life in the Protestant churches. Ramm sees it as a movement in continuity with Protestant Orthodoxy, but rid of some of Orthodoxy's rationalistic character. It shares Orthodoxy's "passion to be biblical" (p. 59), and its "goal of precision in theology" (p. 61), but it has much less confidence in systematization in theology and is more modest in its claims to knowledge. In short it is a chastened and liberated orthodoxy.[4]

Understood from this perspective Evangelical theology raises many of the questions which first- and second-generation Anabaptists already faced in their debates with Protestants. A basis for dialogue between the two is present, however, because Anabaptism and Evangelicalism share a common loyalty to biblical authority and an understanding of salvation by grace through faith. In that basic sense Anabaptism is evangelical to the core. But what are the marks of difference?

First, with some noteworthy modifications Evangelicalism still holds to a spiritualized view of the true church as "invisible." This invisibility has been rendered somewhat less platonic by virtue of circumstances, namely, the legalization of religious voluntaryism. Evangelical congregations tend to be made up of "believers" whose integrity is demonstrated in their faithful support of the church. But Evangelicalism lacks a theology that undergirds a disciples church in which the disciplines of grace are encouraged and expected. Its concept of the church as the instrument of grace is still based upon the presuppositions and definitions of a Calvinistic view of divine election and the invisibility of true faith.

Second, its concepts of salvation remain individualized and privatized. There is some talk about saving whole persons rather than saving souls, but evangelism is still conceived as separate from discipling. The difference between being saved and unsaved is defined in purely "spiritual" terms, and the absolute difference hinges on a theological affirmation of belief in Christ as Savior. Thus by theological definition it is exclusive of social and psychological dimensions.

Anabaptism, by way of contrast, had a concept of the church and salvation that was at once both spiritual and social. To be saved meant to enter into the body of Christ through the voluntary acceptance of "the new covenant in His blood." This is a third alternative to those of classical Protestantism and Roman Catholicism. Ramm identifies Evangelicalism with Protestantism and explains the difference thus: " . . . in Roman Catholic ecclesiology the believer relates himself to the church which in turn relates him to Christ, whereas in Protestantism the believer is directly related to Christ who in turn relates him to the church".[4] Anabaptists held that the believer is saved by Christ in His body. From the human side this required a commitment to the lordship of Christ as head of His body, the church. Theologically salvation was not defined as a relation to Christ (spiritual) prior to and apart from a relation to His body (social). Of course, in the contingencies of time and space there may be consequential priority, but this is not given logical recognition in a theological rationale. On the other hand, neither is it identified with a sacramental relation to the church. Baptism was understood as simultaneously entrance into Christ and His body, the church.

Third, Evangelicalism continues its verbal and rationalistic concept of the Word of God as contained in Scripture, and accordingly it views theological orthodoxy rather than authenticity of the church's life as the criterion of continuity with Christ. Evangelicalism is not overly concerned with the question of authentic community because the continuing witness to the kingdom of God is identified with the written Word and not with the witnessing church. The concern is for a correct inerrant Word.

Thus in this tradition, great importance is attached to theories of verbal inspiration and orthodox statements. The church's responsibility has been understood as preaching an orthodox message which is self-authenticating. This kind of theology shifts the primary focus from Jesus Christ to Scripture as the authenticating reality. The credibility of the contemporary witness does not rest on its Christly authenticity, that is, its participation in the original authoritative Word, but upon inspiration which guarantees Scripture's revelatory character. The credibility of the church's life is not involved.

Anabaptism, on the other hand, has insisted that authentic discipleship is the criterion for continuity with Christ who is the original authority *(authentēs)*. It is concerned with correct understanding and teaching as one function of the church's life, but its primal responsibility is authentic witness as the disciple community. Correct doctrine and understanding is for correct practice. Thus Anabaptist confessions of faith are not viewed as universal orthodox, or dogmatic, statements of the gospel. They are rather statements of the working consensus of the group, and they are open to revision by ongoing consensus.

Fourth, Evangelical theology has no clear-cut critique of American culture. Its theology and ethics continue to be closely allied with a nationalistic political rationale. This shows up first in ethics and in social and political attitudes, but these are based firmly on theological presuppositions and definitions. For example, concepts of justice which call for revenge upon the criminal and even the death penalty are grounded in a theological concept of God's justice. I have recently seen an extreme example of this which used the orthodox penal substitution theory of atonement to justify and advocate the death penalty for crime. Other examples include a theological view of God that justifies America's affluence as the blessing of a benign national deity, and views American military power as God's protective arm for missionaries and the forces of righteousness. (See Romans 2:3-5 for a biblical denunciation of such ego-centered heresy.)

In this respect Evangelical theology stands in continuity with Protestant Orthodoxy. Orthodoxy spelled out the uniform doctrine for an established church. Its religious belief system was coordinate to the sacramental values of the realm. Its whole system was oriented to and supportive of the established government and economic elite. It furnished the theological rationale for the state as a "Christian" government. Our attention has been called anew to this aspect of European and North American theological systems by some of the contemporary South American theologians. And their point is well taken. One gets the impression that even yet some major proponents of contemporary North American Evangelicalism have no objection to its becoming the national civil religion.

Robert Webber, Theology professor at Wheaton College, has written, "What is needed now, is a theological corrective of such a nature that the Evangelical church will be shed of her social, political, and cultural identification. We need a corrective that will allow Christ to emerge through the church's worship, theology, mission, and spirituality as the hope of the world."[5]

By contrast, Anabaptism was just such a theological corrective! As we have noted it was a radical, prophetic-evangelistic critique and call for action in the name of Jesus Christ.

Radical Evangelicals

For our purposes it is not necessary to compare all the various positions within Evangelicalism and Anabaptism. However, within Quebedeaux's classification of "New Evangelicals" one group merits attention. These radical, and for the most part younger, leaders, which he calls "Young Evangelicals," are challenging established Evangelical positions on the basis of their own presuppositions and claims. In the name of radical biblicism they are calling Evangelicals to a more rigorous discipleship. Those with a charismatic bent are calling them to a more radical experience of the Holy Spirit's power and to a more *koinoniac* model of the church as the loving community.[6] Others press the need for a consistent biblical critique of contemporary culture and more radical action to demonstrate the justice of the kingdom of God.[7] And there are others who beckon them to "the new community" as a fundamental aspect of holistic witness.[8]

If we compare Anabaptism with these groups, we find much that is compatible between the two. Indeed, many of these Evangelicals have been directly influenced by the writings of neo-Anabaptist writers who are both interpreting the historical movement and attempting to relate it to the current theological dialogue. The commonalities are almost self-evident: a radical disassociation from and critique of nationalistic religion and politics, adoption of a witness lifestyle which demonstrates as well as verbalizes the gospel of the kingdom, a strong sense of urgency for remedial action now, and a consistent emphasis on nonviolence.

Anabaptism cannot be identified with any denominational tradition—not even those who claim direct lineal descent from the original movement. Institutionalization of a movement tends to freeze issues and forms so that with the passage of time and changes in the cultural situation their original meaning and significance are lost. Neither can Anabaptism be unequivocally identified with any radical religious protest today if for no other reason than that the historical situation is so very different. But its spirit lives on in those prophetic disciples who have seen anew the vision of a new creation in Christ and bear uncompromising witness to His lordship.

Notes

Chapter 1

1. James DeFrost Murch, *Cooperation Without Compromise* (Grand Rapids: Eerdmans, 1956).

2. See John R. W. Stott, "Forward from Lausanne," *Christianity Today*, June 2, 1978, p. 28.

3. *Religion in America: The Gallup Opinion Index*, 1977-78, Report No. 145 (Princeton, N.J.: The American Institute of Public Opinion, 1978), p. 41. There are a number of very interesting data in this report. The pollsters give the following definition of what it means to be evangelical: "(1) has had a born again conversion, (2) accepts Jesus as his or her personal Savior, (3) believes the Scriptures are the authority for all doctrine, and (4) feels an urgent duty to spread the faith" (*Ibid.*, p. 49). There are an estimated 40 million adults in the U.S.A. that describe themselves as "evangelical." About 3,000,000 are part of the charismatic movement. The discrepency between 34 percent who say they are "born again" and "have tried to encourage someone to believe in Jesus Christ" and the 28 percent who say they are "evangelical" indicates an uncertainty in peoples' minds about the term evangelical. If we take the "born again" figure, then some 50 million Americans 18 years of age and above are by profession evangelical Christians. Of that group 57 percent are 50 or older and 77 percent are white.

4. See *Christianity Today*, November 4, 1977, pp. 51, 52.

5. See wallis and Michaelson, "The Plan to Save America," *Sojourners*, April 1976. Also see the October 1976 issue on the "Election '76."

Chapter 3

1. Charles Edwin Jones, *Perfectionist Persuasion: The Holiness Movement and American Methodism, 1867-1936* (Metuchen, N.J.: Scarecrow Press, 1974) tells the story.

2. Vinson Synan, *The Holiness-Pentecostal Movement* (Grand Rapids: Eerdmans, 1971), pp. 61, 62.

3. Rodman Williams, *The Pentecostal Reality* (Plainfield, N.J.: Logos, 1972), writes sympathetically of this new movement.

4. Frederick Dale Bruner, *A Theology of the Holy Spirit* (Grand Rapids: Eerdmans, 1970), pp. 76 ff.

Chapter 5

1. William G. McLoughlin, ed., *The American Evangelicals 1800-1900* (New York: Harper and Row, 1968), p. 1.

2. Richard Pierard, *The Unequal Yoke: Evangelical Christianity and Political Conservatism* (Philadelphia: J. B. Lippincott, 1970), p. 21.

3. Alexis de Tocqueville *Democracy in America* (New York: A. A. Knopf, 1945), Volume I, p. 305.

4. *Ibid.*, p. 800.

5. Albert J. Menendez, *Religion at the Polls* (Philadelphia: Westminster Press, 1977), p. 103.

6. *South Bend Tribune*, December 12, 1977, p. 18.

7. *Op. cit.*, p. 198 and 188.

8. Jim Wallis and Wes Michaelson, "The Plan to Save America," *Sojourners* April 1976, p. 11.

9. *Ibid.*, p. 9.

10. John H. Redekop, *The American Far Right: A Case Study of Billy James Hargis* (Grand Rapids: Eerdmans, 1968), p. 43.

11. *Christianity Today*, July 31, 1970, p. 21.

12. *Op. cit.*, p. 17.

13. *Op. cit.*, p. 43.

14. Richard Quebedeaux, *The Worldly Evangelicals* (San Francisco: Harper and Row, 1978), p. 83.

15. Quoted by S. M. Lipset in Robert Lee and Martin Marty, eds., *Religion and Social Conflict* (New York: Oxford University Press, 1969), p. 84.

16. David F. Wells and John D. Woodbridge, eds., *The Evangelicals* (Nashville: Abingdon, 1975), p. 23.

17. Quoted in Martin Marty, *A Nation of Behavers* (Chicago: University of Chicago Press, 1976), p. 92.

18. Erling Jorstad, *The Politics of Doomsday: Fundamentalists of*

the Far Right (Nashville: Abingdon, 1970), p. 15.

19. Marty, *op. cit.*, p. 105.

20. *Op. cit.*, p. 202.

21. *Op. cit.*, p. 174.

Chapter 6

1. "Docetic" comes from a Greek word that means to seem, to think. A docetic view of Christ makes Him only seem to be human, and likewise a docetic view of Scripture would make them only seem to be human.

2. Writing in the *New Catholic Encyclopedia*, J. T. Forestell remarks: "The metaphor of the musical instrument is common among the Fathers but tends to minimize the role of the human author."

3. *Epistle* 82, 1, 3.

4. *New Catholic Encyclopedia*.

5. *Edwin A. Burtt, Types of Religious Philosophy* (New York: Harper, 1938), pp. 302 ff.

6. A good summary of this point of view is in J. A. Bewer, *The Literature of the Old Testament in its Historical Development*, 1924, and in Robert H. Pfeiffer, *Introduction to the Old Testament*, 1941.

7. As an example of a modernist work note the book *The Faith of Modernism* by Shailer Mathews written in 1924.

8. *The Fundamentals, A Testimony, Volume XII* (Testimony Publishing Company, 1914), pp. 4-8.

9. Schaff, *Creeds of Christendom III* (Harper, 1877), pp. 602, 603.

Chapter 7

1. Carl F. H. Henry, ed., *Prophecy in the Making* (Carol Stream, Ill.: Creation House, 1971).

2. See Clarence Bass, *Backgrounds to Dispensationalism* (Grand Rapids: Eerdmans, 1960); Oswald Allis, *Prophecy and the Church* (Philadelphia: Presbyterian and Reformed Publishing Co., 1945); Eldon Ladd, *The Presence of the Future* (Grand Rapids: Eerdmans, 1974); C. Norman Kraus, *Dispensationalism in America* (Richmond, John Knox Press, 1958); Ernest Sandeen, *The Roots of Fundamentalism* (Chicago: University of Chicago Press, 1970).

3. Charles Caldwell Ryrie, *Dispensationalism Today* (Chicago: Moody Press, 1965).

4. Ernest Lee Tuveson, *Millennium and Utopia* (New York: Harper and Row, 1949, 1964); Clark Garrett, *Respectable Folly* (Baltimore: Johns Hopkins, 1975).

5. Tuveson, pp. 26, 27, 28.

6. Tuveson, p. 92.

7. Tuveson, p. 88.

8. Tuveson, pp. 77, 78.

9. Tuveson, p. 79.

10. *Ibid.*

11. Good books have been written on the meaning of apocalyptic literature such as Ezekiel, Daniel, and Revelation: Klaus Koch, *The Rediscovery of Apocalyptic* (Naperville: A. R. Allenson, 1972); Leon Morris, *Apocalyptic* (Grand Rapids: Eerdmans, 1972); H. H. Rowley, *The Relevance of Apocalyptic* (London: Lutterworth Press, 1944); Walter Schmithals, *The Apocalyptic Movement* (Nashville: Abingdon Press, 1975).

12. See Bernard Anderson, *Understanding the Old Testament,* second edition (Englewood Cliffs: Prentice-Hall, 1966), p. 545.

13. C. Norman Kraus, *The Community of the Spirit* (Grand Rapids: Eerdmans, 1974), p. 94.

14. *Mennonite Encyclopedia* (Scottdale, Pa.: Herald Press, 1955).

15. *Ibid.*

Chapter 8

1. For one attempt to develop this argument, see my "A Call for Evangelical Nonviolence," *Christian Century,* September 15, 1976, pp. 753-757.

2. See my *Evangelism, Salvation and Social Justice* (Grove Booklets, 1977).

3. John Howard Yoder, *Politics of Jesus* (Grand Rapids: Eerdmans, 1973), p. 134.

4. Charles E. Raven in Rufus H. Jones, ed., *The Church, The Gospel, and War* (New York: Harper, 1948), p. 5.

5. *Christianity Today,* March 28, 1975, pp. 41, 42.

6. By discussing Yoder at this point, I do *not* mean that I consider his chapter on the Pauline doctrine of justification heretical! I treasure Yoder as one of my foremost teachers and consider his *Politics* one of the most important evangelical publications of the last decade. But I do think Chapter 11 displays an unnecessary tendency to stress the ethical and social at the expense of the vertical aspects of Christian faith.

7. Yoder, *Politics of Jesus,* p. 218.

8. *Ibid.,* p. 223.

9. Werner Foerster, "Eirene," *Theological Dictionary of the New Testament,* ed. Gerhard Kittei and trans. Geoffrey W. Bromley (Grand Rapids: Eerdmans, 1964 ff.), Vol. II, p. 415.

10. Romans 5:1. Kittel's dictionary indicates that one must understand peace here solely in a forensic way; *ibid.*

11. See also Acts 11:1-18.

12. See further my "Jesus' Resurrection and Radical Discipleship," *Right On*, April 1976.

13. James Douglas, *The Non-Violent Cross: A Theology of Revolution and Peace* (New York: Macmillan, 1968), pp. 23, 24. Douglas is a Roman Catholic lay theologian who has espoused radical pacifism.

14. Gordon D. Kaufman, *Systematic Theology: A Historicist Perspective* (New York: Scribner's, 1968), p. 422.

15. *Ibid.*, p. 426.

16. See my "The Historian, The Miraculous and Post-Newtonian Man," *Scottish Journal of Theology*, XXV (1972), 309-319; "St. Paul's Understanding of the Nature and Significance of the Resurrection in 1 Corinthians 15:1-19," *Novum Testamentum*, XIX (1977), 124-141; "The Pauline Conception of the Resurrection Body in 1 Corinthians 15:35-54," *New Testament Studies*, XXI (1976), 428-439.

17. John Updike, "Seven Stanzas at Easter," *Verse: The Carpentered Hen and Other Tame Creatures. . . .* (New York: Fawcett Publications, 1965), p. 164.

18. Probably a majority of Mennonites fall into this group.

Chapter 9

1. Art Gish, *The New Left and Christian Radicalism* (Grand Rapids, Mich.: Eerdmans, 1970), p. 66.

2. Richard Quebedeaux, *The Young Evangelicals* (New York, N.Y.: Harper & Row, 1974).

3. Bernard Ramm, *The Evangelical Heritage* (Waco, Tex.: Word Books, 1973). Kanzer has a definitive article in Wells and Woodbridge, *The Evangelicals* (Nashville, Tenn.: Abingdon Press, 1975).

4. Ramm, *ibid.*, p. 37.

5. "To Recover Our Apostolic Roots," *The New Oxford Review*, January 1978, p. 13.

6. Graham Pulkingham, *Gathered for Power* (Wilton, Conn.: Morehouse-Barlow, 1972); *They Left Their Nets* (Wilton, Conn.: Morehouse-Barlow, 1973).

7. See James Wallis, *Agenda for a Biblical People* (New York, N.Y.: Harper & Row, 1976), and John Perkins, *A Quiet Revolution* (Waco, Tex.: Word Books, 1976).

8. Elizabeth O'Connor, *The New Community* (New York, N.Y.: Harper & Row, 1976). Howard A. Snyder, *The Community of the King* (Downers Grove, Ill.: Inter-Varsity Press, 1977).

C. Norman Kraus is a professor of religion and director of the Center for Discipleship at Goshen College. A student of both Anabaptism and Evangelicalism and its origins, he is the author of *Dispensationalism in America* (John Knox, 1958) and book review editor of the *Mennonite Quarterly Review*.

A native of Newport News, Virginia, Kraus earned graduate degrees from Princeton Theological Seminary and Duke University (PhD). Aside from numerous articles, he is also the author of *Dispensationalism In America: Its Rise and Development* (John Knox, 1958), *The Healing Christ* (Herald Press, 1971), *The Community of the Spirit* (Eerdmans, 1974), and *The Authentic Witness* (Eerdmans, 1979).

A Mennonite minister, he is a member of the Assembly

congregation at Goshen, Indiana, and presently serves on the overseas committee of the denomination's board of missions. He has been active in teaching missions in churches in India, Japan, Indonesia, the Philippines, and various East African countries.